URBAN FARES POLICY

Urban Fares Policy

ALEXANDER GREY

SAXON HOUSE | LEXINGTON BOOKS

Published by

SAXON HOUSE, D. C. Heath Ltd.
Westmead, Farnborough, Hants., England.

Jointly with

LEXINGTON BOOKS, D. C. Heath & Co.
Lexington, Mass. USA.

ISBN 0 347 01090 3

Library of Congress Catalog Card Number 75–28614

Printed in Great Britain by Butler & Tanner Ltd., Frome and London

Contents

List of tables

List of figures

Preface

This book explores a number of issues concerned with how public transport services in towns should be charged for. Rural and inter-city services are not considered in their own right, though many of the arguments and conclusions might be applicable there as well. Although written from a practical standpoint, an attempt has been made to unravel certain theoretical issues as well, with the aim of at least partly narrowing the gap between theory and practice that exists in so many disciplines.

I hope that the book will be of interest to lay readers as well as to academics and professionals working in the field. Indeed, in one important respect everyone is an expert in transport planning, their expertise being derived from daily personal experiences of how various parts of the transport system actually work. But unfortunately this advantage also accentuates the difficulties of taking decisions in transport planning as well as in many other areas of social policy. One person's view can easily be challenged by another's, and this sometimes encourages opinion and judgement to dominate (instead of to interact with and be influenced by) logic and evidence in discussions of important policy issues.

The use of mathematics in the social as well as in the physical sciences is a good way of resolving that dilemma, for mathematics is an invaluable tool for checking the consistency of opinions with each other and with the evidence, as well as for exposing and highlighting them for what they are. But in adopting such an approach it is important to guard against using mathematics (together with unnecessary technical jargon) not as a lantern to illuminate the argument, but as a smokescreen to disguise it. I have tried (though not always successfully) to avoid that trap by putting most of the mathematics and technical matter in appendices. The main exception is Chapter 4, which many lay readers may prefer to skip as it is concerned primarily with detailed technical issues which should be of greater interest to academics and professionals.

Most of the ideas in the book have arisen from discussions with colleagues in the course of my work over the last couple of years and with other friends during what has been an unusually stimulating and enjoyable period. I have particularly valued the many discussions with those who have explained the traditional approaches to urban transport planning problems and who, I am sure, will take my criticisms of certain views and methods in good part. Transport planners and others whose thoughts and technical advice I have learned from are far too numerous to mention individually, but I am especially grateful for helpful comments on earlier drafts of some or all of the chapters to David Bayliss, Malcolm Buchanan, Paul Godier, Phil Goodwin, David Lewis, Paul Mullen, Ian Phillips and Roger Webber. David Lewis made a substantial contribution to Chapter 6, being responsible for the extraction and computer analysis of the data used to construct the statistical equations, and joint author of the article from which the chapter was developed.* For the same chapter, the Department of Employment were extremely helpful in providing hitherto unpublished information from the Family Expenditure Surveys for 1972 and 1973. Sandra Massara showed exceptional patience and efficiency in providing general assistance and in typing both prose and mathematics from scripts which most people would have been unable to decipher. Finally, my deepest debt of gratitude is due to my wife Eleanor, who not only put up cheerfully with six months of disruption to family life, but also helped to improve the book's style and correct a number of logical errors in earlier drafts.

If in spite of all this helpful advice the book still contains mistakes or fails to deal adequately with important topics, such errors and omissions are entirely my responsibility. It should also be stressed that all opinions put forward are my own personal views and do not reflect those of the Greater London Council.

Alexander Grey
June 1975

---

* Public Transport Fares and the Public Interest, *Town Planning Review*, July 1975.

1 The Changing Emphasis in Transport Planning

A quarter of a century ago many cities in Europe were recovering from the ravages of war, with comparatively low living standards, food restrictions, and damaged and decayed urban fabric. But for those who could afford it, it was easy to move around from one part of the city to another. Those fortunate enough to own a car could drive little hindered by other traffic and unaffected by parking restrictions or complicated traffic management schemes. And public transport on the whole provided a frequent and reliable service. But today, although average real incomes per head in most industrialised countries (even the United Kingdom) have at least doubled, travel in many towns can be a harrowing experience. The public image is that car drivers are harassed by fines and traffic regulations that seem to do nothing except create extra frustration and inconvenience for everyone. People feel that they have to put up with waiting at the bus stop for the bus which never seems to come except in a convoy, hampered as it is by staff and spare part shortages as well as by traffic jams. And travellers to and from work often have to endure being squashed together in overcrowded buses and trains during the rush hours.

In case it should seem that traffic congestion and associated environmental pollution are wholly modern phenomena, it is worth noting that the largest stage coach company in Great Britain had around 150,000 horses in 1830. But in the latter half of the twentieth century transport problems have been intensified and the previous situation of comparatively low living standards but good transport has been stood on its head. This is largely because rising incomes have made it possible for more and more people to buy and use what is to each of them individually by far the quickest, most convenient, comfortable, flexible and personal form of transport, but which causes for society the gravest problems of social and environmental management: namely the car.

The benefits derived by the individual motorist from using his car in a town can be far more important to him than the costs he incurs, even when the difficulties of driving in congested city centres are taken into account. But the costs to society of the actions of all motorists taken together can be far greater than the sum of the costs they each incur as

1

individuals. By comparison with the bus, which for carrying passengers from one point to another uses scarce road space much more efficiently (at least with normal peak period loadings)[1] the extra social costs created by cars in city centres include more accidents; more noise and fumes; longer and more unreliable travelling times; and greater inconvenience and danger to cyclists and pedestrians.

The increasing importance of the car in transport planning is illustrated in Figure 1.1. This shows that the number of cars in use in Great Britain nearly quintupled between 1953 and 1973, and that the total distance covered by car drivers was nearly six times greater by the end of that twenty year period.

Fig. 1.1 Increase in cars in use, distance travelled, and road expenditure Great Britain 1953–73

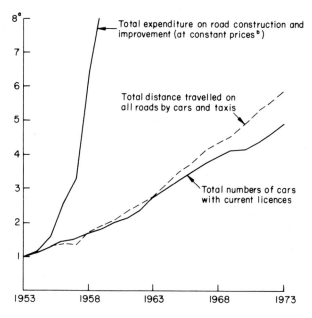

Source: Calculated from Tables 245–7 of *Annual Abstract of Statistics* 1974, and corresponding tables for earlier years

[a] The left hand axis is an index number with the index set at 1 in 1953. Thus the indices 2, 3, 4, etc., are the points at which the quantities shown on the three graphs will have doubled, trebled, quadrupled, etc., from their 1953 values.

[b] The index of the cost of new construction (published in the *Monthly Digest of Statistics*) has been used to convert actual money expenditures on road construction and improvement to expenditures at constant prices.

2

A similar pattern has been observed in other industrialised countries. Until recently, most of them have attempted to cope with the growth in car ownership and use by a vast expansion in road planning and building, spearheaded particularly in the United States by their massive road programmes as well as by the development in the 1950s of new methods of transport planning designed primarily to assist the planning of new roads. In Great Britain, the expenditure on road construction in 1972–73 was over thirty times greater than twenty years earlier if the figures are corrected for inflation by being expressed in terms of constant prices. It grew from £8·4 million in 1953 to £261·1 million in 1972/73 at constant 1953 prices — which is why that line goes off the map in Figure 1.1. The fastest rate of growth was during the 1950s, expenditure (at constant prices) being over eight times greater in 1960 than in 1953. But the growth continued at a rapid pace during the 1960s to reach its peak in 1970 when the real expenditure had multiplied by another four times. Expressed in actual money prices the growth continued after 1970, with the actual expenditure in 1972–73 being £537·9 million — more than sixty times greater than in 1953.

But the problems still remain, and new social and economic pressures make it very difficult to continue to try to tackle them through the road building solution. Before discussing the nature of these pressures and the proposed new solutions, it is worth contrasting them with the conventional approach that has developed from the road building background.

1.1   Conventional transport planning

The methods of transport planning which grew up in the United States in the 1950s are now used as standard practice in several industrialised countries: particularly for urban and regional transport planning studies in the United States and in the United Kingdom.

This conventional process can be divided into the three separate aspects which are shown in the flow diagram in Figure 1.2 and summarised in the discussion which follows.[2]

1   *Problem definition* This is the start of the process. It begins by defining the boundaries of the study area and dividing it into a number of zones for geographical analysis. Detailed information is collected by desk research and from special surveys about the characteristics of the area, of the people who live and work there and their travelling habits, and of the

Fig. 1.2   The conventional transport planning process

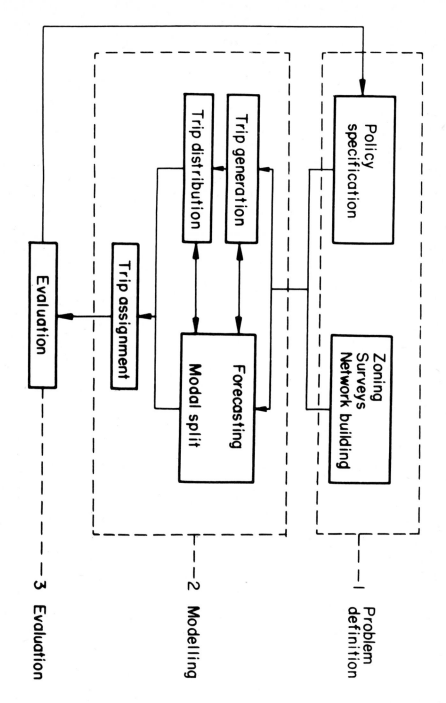

4

transport facilities provided. The transport system is defined and coded for computer analysis as a network of nodes and links between them, with the nodes related to the centres of gravity of all trips generated in or attracted to each zone. The transport policies to be modelled and evaluated at the subsequent stages are also specified.

2 *Modelling* In this stage, which is the core of the whole process, models are constructed so as to simulate the way in which people behave as revealed by the data collection exercises carried out in the first stage, and to estimate how this behaviour will change in response to changes in the underlying assumptions. This is done in three sequential steps. The first is *trip generation,* at which the total number of trips starting or ending in each zone is estimated, usually either by rough back-of-the-envelope calculations, or by simple statistical models. A technique called category analysis, which has been developed by transport planners especially for this purpose, is also sometimes used.

The total number of trips estimated in this way is then spread over the whole network in the *trip distribution* stage. A table known as a *trip matrix* is constructed, in which each entry (or cell) represents the number of trips originating in one zone and attracted to another. The totals of the rows and columns of the table are the total numbers of trips starting and ending in each zone, as calculated from the trip generation stage. The methods used to build up the table include gravity models and various special *growth factor* models which have again been designed specifically for transport planning.

By the end of this stage two trip matrices are in fact produced; one for public and the other for private transport. The division of the total number of trips into public and private transport components is done by a process known as *modal split,* which is carried out at either the generation or distribution stage, or both. Further, although the number of trips starting and ending in each zone will have originally been estimated for the base year for which the data has been collected, those coming out at the end of the distribution phase will be forecasts of the private and public transport flows for the design year for which the transport plan or policy changes are being considered. These forecasts are also carried out at either the generation or distribution stage, or both.

In calculating modal split another idea that has again been specially developed for transport planning comes into play. This is that travellers will decide how to get around the city according to which form of transport results in the lowest *generalised cost,* defined as a weighted sum of the key factors influencing their behaviour. Travel time and its various components (walking, waiting, and changing time as well as the time

5

actually spent in the car, bus or train) are generally considered to be the most important of these factors.

In addition, many models now include the money costs of travel (public transport fares as well as the real cost of using a private car for the journey). Consideration has also been given to the best way of including other factors like comfort and reliability, but with little success to date. It is important to note that the weights used in defining generalised cost from its various components are usually not derived directly from the data used to construct the model, but taken as given from an outside source. In Britain, the generalised cost weights used in most transport planning models are standard values recommended by the Department of the Environment.

The third step is known as *trip assignment*, which refers to the process of separately assigning the number of trips made by private and public transport to specific paths through the road network in the former case, and specific bus routes and railway lines and services in the latter. As with modal split, trips are assigned to individual paths on the assumption that people will minimise the generalised cost of their travel between any two points.

3 *Evaluation* The alternative policies that are considered in the conventional transport planning process are normally those that have a big impact on reducing travel time between any two zones in the network — such as building a new road or railway line. These options will lead to different predictions of passenger flows on individual routes and services over the whole network. In the evaluation phase these demands are compared with the costs of the policies which create them, using primarily a form of cost-benefit analysis which incorporates once again the generalised cost concept.

1.2 Problems with the conventional approach

A prime feature of the conventional approach is its geographical base, which is a necessary consequence of the nature of the problems it was developed to handle. The approach reflects not only the highway engineer's justifiable concern with the effect of transport decisions on total traffic flows on specific roads in specific parts of the city, but also the fact that the effects of decisions on road construction and widening are felt only at specific locations. In fares policy, however, and in some other areas of transport policy, the effects of a new decision are usually felt in all parts of the city at the same time. The general information required to assist fares policy decisions concerns matters such as the potential impact on total receipts, and on the distribution of income between rich and poor people: neither of which is easily handled by the conventional model. Moreover, people will react to and be affected by the policy change more according to who they are than where they live; whether they are shoppers, pensioners, children, rich or poor, with or without a car, and so on. Thus the detailed information needed for fares policy decisions concerns social classifications of that kind rather than geographical analyses.

Yet the conventional model is already so complex in its geographical structure that further classifications by social structure are very difficult to handle. In the transport planning model being developed by the Greater London Council, for example, 945 zones have had to be drawn up to give a reasonable geographical coverage, which means that each of the two matrices for total public and private transport trips has not far short of a million cells. Thus there would either be insufficient data to allow reliable social analyses to be carried out (the cell sizes would be too small), or an enormously expensive and cumbersome data collection exercise would have to be mounted. And in either case very complicated analytical routines would be needed.

In fact the data collection problems are formidable enough even if further social analyses are not required. This means that any urban authority can only afford to launch the new surveys needed for updating the model after a long period has elapsed since the previous exercise. Thus it is difficult to prevent the model from becoming cumbersome, sluggish and unresponsive to the flexible and dynamic requirements of some areas of transport planning. This is not such a problem when large capital investments, which take a long time to be constructed, are being considered. Fares policy decisions, however, can be taken and implemented very quickly, and must therefore be supported by flexible and interactive analytical routines of the kind that are not provided by the conventional model.

Fortunately, these problems are not nearly as severe now as they were a decade or so ago. For the traditional procedures have been developed hand in hand with considerable improvements in computer programming and systems analysis, so that large volumes of data can now be handled comparatively quickly and easily. But this strength is at the same time a weakness, for it tends to make the whole process even more dependent on the computer, with computer running time often having to be the main constraint affecting how a particular piece of analysis can be done. Category analysis, for example, is really an adulterated form of the dummy variable technique used in econometrics. And although it has therefore lost much of the rigour and consistency provided by a well established statistical technique, such drawbacks are offset by the considerable simplifications to the computational process that are made possible. As another example, it has been suggested that the conventional approach to modal split (with trips first divided between private and public transport in the generation and distribution phases, and then split between bus and train in the assignment phase) may be partly explained by the fact that computer programs for calibrating multinomial models were developed later than programs for binary models.[3] To put it another way, it could be argued that relatively straightforward computer programming has been considered more important than the advantages that might be gained from a simultaneous approach to distribution and assignment.

This is part of a wider problem with the conventional approach, caused by the process of breaking down the transport planning process into various separate aspects which are treated sequentially in a way which makes it impossible to consider interactions between things that happen unless they occur at precisely the same stage in the chosen sequence. Thus the overall demand for travel is usually estimated at the trip generation stage independently of the effect of building (say) a new road network. The implications of such a policy are only considered explicitly at the distribution and assignment phases. This ignores the interaction between demand and supply, and makes it impossible for the conventional approach to analyse, for instance, the extent to which the additional traffic generated by a new or widened road will absorb the extra road capacity. Moreover, the omission of supply parameters will lead to erroneous estimates of demand not only because they influence demand directly, but also because they may be related to other independent variables that are used to estimate demand. For example, the amount of road capacity available could in due course influence the amount of car ownership, which is an independent variable often used to estimate demand in the trip generation stage.

A more defensible approach would be to use the relevant statistical techniques to investigate simultaneously the interaction between demand, supply and the other factors influencing demand. As an example of such an approach, Feldstein's study of the British National Health Service[4] showed that providing enough hospital beds to keep pace with demand was a limitless goal since demand appeared to reflect closely the available supply. He therefore devised a method of analysis which could be used to estimate the interaction between all the various influences on demand and supply including the effects of the policy maker's own decisions — employing standard econometric techniques which are not at present used in transport planning.

These remarks have indicated another major problem with the conventional approach: that it is much too dependent on intuitions and judgements that get hidden within the analytical process itself, without having the checks and balances that would have been provided if the normal rules of statistical method had been observed. In other words, there is a strong temptation to cook the books. This arises not only in the temptation to create special techniques like modal split and category analysis, as already mentioned, but also in other areas. In the assignment stage, for example, a large number of estimated flows on individual routes or lines have to be matched with observed data, using no more than a computer algorithm based on the minimum generalised cost hypothesis. If a predicted flow on any section is right out of line with observed data, it is difficult for the analyst to avoid making intuitive adjustments to either the network or the trip table in the relevant zone or zones.

Actually the generalised cost concept itself prevents the model from giving the best estimates of passenger flows on the network. This is beause the weights which define generalised cost are usually predetermined, and the model is set up by seeing how generalised cost (rather than its components) relates to the observed data. As a result the model is logically bound to correspond less well with the empirical evidence (whatever statistical criterion is chosen) than if the relationships had been estimated directly from the variables that are assumed to influence travel behaviour. The only exception would arise if the relative importance of these influences, as revealed by the process of direct estimation, happened to be the same as the weights that are used to combine them into generalised cost. This is most unlikely to be the case in Britain, where the Department of the Environment's recommended values for the generalised cost weights are derived from cost benefit and consumer surplus assumptions (see p. 27) which require the time people spend travelling to be valued in relation to their incomes. Specific social biases are thereby introduced, which are not necessarily related to the way people actually behave.

Fortunately several of the modal split models that have been constructed and applied do not have these drawbacks, since the explanatory variables have been related directly to the observed data using well established statistical techniques.[5] But if the relative influences of the components of generalised cost are estimated in this way, it is highly misleading to make use of the term: for in those circumstances it becomes an abstract concept which adds nothing (except confusion) to what is revealed in the process of direct estimation and reinforces the book cooking temptations. If generalised cost were dropped from the transport planner's vocabulary, it would ease the process of constructing a better model, and help focus attention on the important facts of life in policy development − namely those variables which influence travel behaviour and can be affected by policy instruments. In particular, the impact of fares changes would be modelled directly instead of being submerged in the misleading generalised cost artefact.

Finally, it should be noted that the computer in the transport planning process is used to simulate, rather than test hypotheses about, human behaviour. Associated with the other problems discussed above, this aspect has led to an almost ontological approach to transport modelling. Thus it has been said that the transport model 'attempts to describe the travel patterns of large numbers of people . . . and can be considered a description of the decision making process the average person might be expected to use when he considers making a journey'.[6] This seems to be in conflict with the approach in most other social sciences, where the purpose of constructing a model is to predict how people will react to changed circumstances (and particularly where they result from new policy decisions), rather than to describe how they currently behave. These predictions, moreover, are not absolute laws about human behaviour, but hypotheses for testing against (and perhaps refuting) empirical evidence.

1.3   Changing economic conditions

The combined effects of the economic recession, the energy crisis and the high inflation that were triggered off by the Arab-Israeli war of October 1973, began in the following year to slow down and even reverse the trends identified earlier. For example, the total distance travelled by car drivers in Great Britain actually fell in 1974 by some 3 per cent, compared with the average compound growth rate of over 9 per cent per annum over 1953−73. The only other recorded fall (of some 2 per cent) took place between 1956 and 1957, and was probably caused by the Suez incident of 1956. As for the number of cars with current licences, the uninterrupted growth continued in 1974 − but the 1974 figure was only 1 per cent higher than in 1973, which is the lowest growth rate for the last twenty years. The average compound growth rate between 1953 and 1973 was over 8 per cent per annum. This and other evidence suggests that people first adapted to the new economic situation by travelling less often or over shorter distances in their cars, and that this initial reaction was followed by a restraining influence on people's attitudes to car ownership as well.

These checks on the growth in demand were matched by even more substantial restraints on the supply side. Public authorities were forced through shortage of funds to switch their attention from large capital investments in the expansion of the system to low cost projects which aim to get the best returns out of maintaining and modernising the assets and operations that already exist.

Whilst it should always have been mere common sense to give priority to low cost–high benefit projects, in the transport field it required a sharp change in the traditional approach to planning and decision making. Instead of the old pattern of demand for road space following supply in an upward spiral, the emphasis had to shift to getting the best use out of the roads that were there. Road building to accommodate cars had to be replaced by traffic restraint to induce people to leave them behind. And public transport planning had to become less concerned with building new railway lines than with improving the speed, comfort and reliability of the existing bus and train services.

More generally, the emphasis began to switch from traffic to people, a point whose significance was highlighted at a time of high inflation and economic recession. For when real incomes are rising, public authorities are faced with what is essentially a comparatively simple monitoring task – namely to see that these gains are distributed between different groups of people in a way that reflects the authorities' social and economic objectives. But when real incomes are falling, more positive actions are required in order to help alleviate and redistribute the extra hardship that may be suffered by some sections of the community. Fares policy could have a major role to play in that process.

1.4 Changing social awareness

In the early 1970s many individuals, pressure groups and government bodies became increasingly concerned with the impact of transport policies on minority groups. It was felt that while the traditional policies might improve the lot of the active, male, employed members of the community travelling to and from work, they often at the same time made travel even more difficult for those who were already much worse off. A road widening scheme, for example, could benefit car drivers while making it very difficult for the housewife without access to a car to cross the road with her children to visit friends or go shopping. Again, replacing lifts with escalators at railway stations would enable most people to get to work more quickly, yet cut the service off altogether from the disabled traveller.

Such anxieties came on top of a more general concern about the housing loss, environmental damage and disruptive effects on local communities of urban road building. Many people now feel that we have come to be obsessed with the problems of transport and traffic in urban areas, at the expense of giving adequate consideration to other community problems. Conventional transport planning studies are heavily dependent on the computer, require large volumes of new data to be collected, and must have a considerable amount of attention, even devotion, to carry them through. Although no comparative figures are available, it is clear that expenditure by government bodies on these conventional studies has considerably exceeded the amounts spent on research in other areas of public policy like housing, education and the personal social services. Moreover, the way in which local authorities are organised lays considerable stress on the importance of linking transport with land-use planning activities, often having them combined in the same department. Yet the equally important links with other areas of public policy often appear to be ignored.

For these reasons a change in emphasis is required, involving a more complete understanding of the social problems of cities. Mobility should be considered as a social need to be met in the context of a vigorous and integrated attack on the more pressing social disadvantages and problems found in other fields.

1.5 Conclusions

These arguments may at first sight seem to imply that the conventional transport planning procedures are wholly inappropriate in the new economic and social climate. But such a conclusion would deny the lessons that have been learned by transport planners from the large amount of development work that has been undertaken in order to extend the conventional procedures from their original road building base. Moreover, although transport decisions are much less concerned with road construction than they were when the conventional procedures were first invented, the policy maker still has to know about the physical effects of these decisions at specific locations. He needs to be able to estimate how actual traffic flows will proceed through the road network as a result of any new decision, and the computer-based transport model could provide him with a useful tool for that purpose.

Perhaps the main implication of the criticisms of the conventional model outlined earlier is that it should not try to incorporate levels of sophistication that it was not designed to bear. In particular, it could be argued that the conventional model should be used principally to test policy changes that have their main impact on travelling time. (In the past these changes would have concerned building new roads and railway lines, but they are now more likely to involve traffic restraint measures like road pricing, and public transport initiatives like the introduction of a network of new express bus services or major interchange improvements.) Further, the computer algorithms used to distribute and assign traffic over the network should be based on travelling time alone, and give up the attempt to incorporate fares as part of the generalised cost concept.

Different procedures should be adopted for the analysis of fares changes and other policies that have special social implications or which influence demand primarily through variables other than travelling time. Technically, this should involve using the appropriate statistical techniques to model directly the effects of policy changes, with the modelling carried out in a flexible and responsive manner using only those variables that are immediately relevant to the decision problem, so that, for example, the effects of transport decisions on specific groups of people can be isolated and analysed. The procedures developed should also take explicit account of the wider political, managerial and social issues surrounding the decision problem, which very often need to be supported by types of mathematical analysis that are quite independent of statistical theory.

The first part of this approach fits in with ideas about direct demand modelling that are now being generated in the United States. It is perhaps not surprising that the country which gave birth to the conventional transport planning process should also be the first to develop substantive criticisms of it; and the new approach to demand modelling in the United States is intended to meet criticisms of the conventional approach similar to those outlined above.[7] But little attention has so far been given to the political and managerial side.

This book attempts to illustrate how an approach covering both of these aspects can be developed for fares policy. The earlier chapters review the practical and theoretical difficulties of taking decisions in a complicated environment and in the face of multiple and conflicting objectives. Some new management solutions are suggested which take account of inflation and of the constitutional and organisational framework within which fares policy decisions have to be taken in many industrialised cities. Current fares initiatives round the world are then described and their implications considered. Finally, by way of example, the impact of different fares policies is analysed in detail for London, concentrating particularly on their social implications.

Notes

[1] 'In terms of road space used and fuel consumed per passenger, a bus remains from 8 to 10 times more efficient than a private car': *London Transport Annual Report* 1974, p. 16.

[2] For a general introduction to the conventional methods, see R. Lane, T. Powell, P. Prestwood Smith, *Analytical Transport Planning,* Duckworth, 1971.

[3] F. de Donnea, *The Determinants of Transport Mode Choice in Dutch Cities,* Rotterdam, 1971, p. 40.

[4] M.S. Feldstein, *Economic Analysis for Health Service Efficiency,* North Holland, 1967.

[5] For a general review of methods of this type, as well as some interesting applications, see F. de Donnea, op.cit.

[6] See R. Lane et al., op.cit., p. 63.

[7] See, for example, D.J. Kulash, *The Mix of Demands,* Urban Institute Working Paper 708–67, Washington, March 1972.

2 The Management of Fares Policy

The management of fares policy involves many different aspects: ranging from communication and control between the bodies responsible for the public transport system as a whole, to detailed operational issues such as the checking and handling of tickets and money. From one town and one country to another there tend to be very different practices for handling these aspects — not surprisingly in view of the differences in culture, constitution, climate, wealth, social structure, and all the other factors that account for the variety and interest of the human race. Nevertheless, it is possible to develop certain common themes and principles which could be used to guide the management of fares policy in most industrialised cities. That is what this chapter attempts to do, drawing mainly on British experience.

2.1 Organisation

The recent reorganisation of local government in Great Britain — which took effect on 1 April 1974 in England and Wales and a year later in Scotland — has given local government major new responsibilities for public transport fares. In England there are now two main tiers of government, counties and districts, with the split of responsibilities in the six main conurbations of Merseyside, Greater Manchester, West Midlands, West Yorkshire, South Yorkshire and Tyne and Wear (the metropolitan areas) somewhat different to that in the rest of the country. Local government in London was unaffected by the reorganisation, but already had a similar pattern of two tier government (the Greater London Council, and thirty-two borough councils plus the City of London) to that in the metropolitan areas, which followed from the earlier reorganisation of London government in 1965. Local government in Wales and Scotland follows a similar pattern, though with the several important differences that are a common feature of British public administration.

In the metropolitan areas in England and Wales, the county councils' responsibilities are predominantly of a strategic nature (e.g. town and country planning), with transport as the only main executive function. But in the nonmetropolitan counties, the county councils (not the districts as in the metropolitan areas) are responsible for two other key executive functions as well: education and the personal social services. Housing is the responsibility of the district councils in both cases, except for certain reserve powers maintained by the counties. The split of responsibilities in London is similar to that in the metropolitan counties, but with two important differences. First, the Greater London Council has major executive responsibilities for housing, which it exercises in parallel with those held by the boroughs. Secondly, education in the thirteen Inner London boroughs is the responsibility of the Inner London Education Authority, which is in effect a subcommittee of the Greater London Council (the elected representatives are the same) but with wholly independent and autonomous powers.

As part of their responsibilities for transport, the six metropolitan county councils in England, and the Strathclyde Regional Council (whose area contains Glasgow) in Scotland, have detailed statutory controls over the level and structure of the fares charged on the public transport services in those areas. Those controls are exercised over the seven Passenger Transport Executives that have been set up to be responsible for the day-to-day management of all public transport services in their areas (apart from those provided by British Rail). The Greater London Council has since 1970 had similar controls over the fares charged by the London Transport Executive, which is responsible for the day-to-day management of London's bus and underground services. In many towns outside the metropolitan areas, the district council itself runs the bus service in accordance with the county council's policy.

Central government, however, still has major direct responsibilities for public transport services and fares in two different areas. First, it takes the final responsibility for the fares charged on all BR's services. However, the metropolitan county councils and the Strathclyde Regional Council can exert some influence through the agreements which they are required to enter into with BR as to what suburban railway services should be provided and how they should be financed.[1] In London, the Greater London Council can also have some influence since BR is required to consult the council each year about both fares and service levels for journeys wholly within Greater London, and to inform them in advance of any proposals for changes of substance.[2] Outside London, the metropolitan counties and the Strathclyde Region, the local authorities have no control over railway fares, though equally there are no towns outside the main conurbations with suburban railway services. Indeed,

16

London is the only conurbation in Great Britain in which there is a substantial amount of suburban railway travel. There is not only the extensive underground system operated by London Transport, but also an equally large suburban network of overground railway services operated by BR. As Table 2.1 shows, nearly a quarter of the people living in Greater London travel to work by train, a much higher proportion than in any of the other conurbations as defined at the time of the 1966 census. Moreover, nearly ten times as many people in Greater London go to work by train as in all the other conurbations combined.

Table 2.1

Means of transport to work in English conurbations
(percentage)

Area of residence	Persons travelling to work by							numbers (=100%)
	train	bus	car	motor cycle	bicycle	foot	other or not stated	
Greater London	23·9	26·5	21·6	2·2	3·9	16·1	5·9	3,858,290
Merseyside	4·7	49·4	19·3	2·3	4·3	15·1	4·8	579,960
Tyneside	3·5	49·5	18·1	1·7	2·5	20·3	4·5	360,760
South East Lancashire	3·0	43·9	21·4	1·9	3·5	19·9	6·4	1,156,090
West Midlands	1·2	40·5	26·0	2·0	4·5	19·9	6·0	1,180,130
West Yorkshire	0·7	47·8	20·6	1·6	1·3	21·5	6·4	816,150

Source: 1966 Sample Census, Workplace and Transport Tables, Part 2, Table 9.

The second major area of central government responsibility is exercised over a large slice of the public transport bus services, through two national holding companies: the National Bus Company for England and Wales, and the Scottish Bus Group. The relative sizes of the responsibilities of the different government bodies and operators are indicated in Table 2.2.

2.2   Management by objectives

Local government reorganisation has been accompanied by a much greater stress on the need to develop management procedures that emphasise the precedence of ends over means and the need to achieve these ends in an

Table 2.2

Bus and coach services in Great Britain — 1973

Operating body	Passenger journeys (million)	Passenger receipts (£ million)	Number of vehicles (end of year)
London Transport Executive	1,439	73·7	6,201
Passenger Transport Executives	1,272	70·6	6,847
Local district councils	2,132	96·1	10,116
Total local government	4,843	240·4	23,164
National Bus Company	2,315	188·0	19,802
Scottish Bus Group	456	41·7	4,540
Total central government	2,771	229·7	24,342
Other operators	830	110·0	26,800

Source: *Annual Abstract of Statistics* 1974, Table 250.

outward looking and flexible manner. These moves towards corporate planning[3] in British local government owe their origin to major developments in theory and practice in the United States in the 1960s, and more recently to active promotion in Britain primarily by the Institute of Local Government Studies at Birmingham. In the private sector, too, there has been a sharp growth in interest in corporate planning and 'management by objectives', the latter being something of an industry in itself. Hence local government managers should no longer need to go as far as the former President of Avis Rent a Car who had a notice on his desk questioning whether actions were getting the firm closer to its objectives, in order to save him 'from a lot of useless trips, lunch dates, conferences, junkets, and meetings'.[4]

Unfortunately the new local government organisation cannot be said to be entirely consistent with these principles, for the two tier system of government has inevitably created new splits in responsibility for closely related programme areas (e.g. housing and personal social services in the nonmetropolitan counties), which is bound to make it more difficult to co-ordinate means to achieve ends. In the transport field, however, local government's responsibilities have been forced at least partly back into the corporate planning mould by new arrangements which require each county council in England and Wales, and the Greater London Council, to submit annually to the Department of the Environment a comprehensive transport plan, known as Transport Policies and Programme, or TPP for short: on the basis of which they each receive a transport block grant for the following financial year as a supplement to the general 'rate support grant' given by central government.

It must be admitted that this new system is not as comprehensive an approach to transport planning as it might have been. As far as public transport is concerned, the main drawback is that the TPPs have to be geared towards those programmes and projects on which the county councils are planning to spend money. This means, for example, that the Greater London Council cannot consider as an integral part of its TPP the substantial network of suburban services operated by BR, and the same applies to the consideration by certain other counties of the major activities of the National Bus Company in their areas. The Department of the Environment has also decided that expenditure on special fares concessions is not eligible for transport supplementary grant (see p. 127).

Nevertheless, the advantages of the new approach are numerous. They include the fact that for the first time revenue projects (including fares) and capital projects have to be appraised together, thus removing the bias towards capital expenditure that existed under the previous arrangements whereby the only grants given by central government were specifically allocated to individual capital projects. Another important feature is that in determining the amount of the transport supplementary grant, the Secretary of State is legally bound to 'have regard to the progress which appears to him to have been made by the council in formulating and implementing suitable policies to meet the needs of their area in connection with transport matters'[5] – thus confirming by statute the current pressures towards management by objectives.

But it is one thing to express management by objectives as an article of faith: quite another to translate it into practical action. This requires not only the formulation of relevant and realistic objectives, but also the specification of procedures to ensure that chosen policies are moving in the right direction and that progress is carefully monitored. Both these aspects raise formidable theoretical and practical difficulties, which are discussed separately below. It will be seen that certain general problems which apply to most management systems are compounded in the area of fares policy by the fact that in the British conurbations (as in many other countries) the responsibility for public transport is shared between governing bodies responsible for policy and overall financial control, and public transport operators responsible for the day-to-day running of the system. Thus the key towards formulating and implementing objectives for fares policy turns upon whether procedures can be found to ensure that these separate responsibilities are recognised in a way that is mutually selfsupporting and makes the maximum contribution to the political authorities' social and economic objectives for the community at large.

2.3 Deciding the objectives

The governing and operating authorities will, of course, need to work out for themselves their objectives for fares policy according to their own political and social beliefs and in the light of the key economic and technical problems that affect public transport operations in their area. But I would suggest four broad principles as guidelines for constructing them.[6] Firstly, the objectives should describe desired future states against which progress can be unambiguously measured. This does not necessarily mean that the aims have to be expressed in numerical terms, which of course will often be neither possible nor appropriate. But it must always be possible to derive from them agreed quantitative measuring rods which can be used to judge, without ambiguity, the extent to which they are being achieved. Hence equivocal concepts like 'fairness' should be avoided unless they can be given a clear definition satisfying these criteria.

Secondly, objectives should be *operable* in the sense that there should be suitable means for achieving them over which the responsible authorities have some control. Thus, for example, although decisions taken by local councils in the United Kingdom are likely to have some indirect influence over the maintenance of industrial and commercial productivity in cities, it would in most cases be inappropriate to express this as one of local government's aims. For the principal means of achieving such an aim would normally lie with firms' own management actions in the context of the trading and fiscal environment determined as a result of central, rather than local, government decisions and controls.

Thirdly, the objectives should be structured according to the normal systems analysis procedure of minimising interaction between, and maximising interaction within, each objective or group of objectives. This principle is concerned with reducing as far as possible the overlaps and duplications that will exist within any collection of objectives, while recognising that it is impossible to make them all mutually exclusive and independent. This would be done, for example, by ensuring that subobjectives which served a similar main objective, or whose implementation required similar management actions (e.g. used the same type of resource or demanded similar kinds of information), were grouped together as far as possible – and vice versa.

20

Finally, the objectives should be constructed in a hierarchical manner with maximum coverage, consistency and relevance at each level. This implies that the local authority should first ensure that its fares policy objectives reflect its wider responsibilities not only for other aspects of transport policy, but also for other public services like housing; then see that they tie in with and are relevant to the operators' responsibilities for the day-to-day management of the public transport services; and finally make sure that they can be translated at lower levels of the hierarchy into detailed quantitative targets related to the actual problems faced 'on the ground'.

Suggestions as to fares policy objectives at the first level in the hierarchy are noted below in four categories. They are intended to reflect the four principles and to apply both to local government and the public transport operator. It should be noted that in order to satisfy the first principle, it is impossible to escape from incorporating values into the objectives. There is no such thing as an 'objective objective' as the direction of the desired change cannot be neutrally determined. The value judgements that have been made are intended to represent a broad consensus of opinion without revealing any particular bias. But it would in principle be quite possible to put an objective such as 1(a) the other way round, so that the aim was to redistribute income from poor to rich people. If this were so all references later on to the 'achievement' of that objective would simply be inverted, sometimes leading to the opposite conclusion to that indicated in the text but without affecting the structure of the argument.

More generally, it should be stressed that this list of objectives has been drawn up purely for the purpose of guiding the discussion, and is not intended to be 'correct' in any sense, nor to indicate priorities.

Illustrative aims for fares policy

1   Social
    (a)   redistribute income from rich to poor people;
    (b)   improve travel opportunities for disadvantaged groups such as the old, the young, the poor, the handicapped, and those without full time access to a private car;
    (c)   reduce overcrowding on public transport vehicles during peak periods;
    (d)   improve frequency, speed and reliability of public transport services;
    (e)   make it more convenient to buy and use tickets.

2 Environmental
   (a)   encourage geographically more compact communities requiring less reliance on transport;
   (b)   encourage movement to the city's strategic centres;
   (c)   reduce traffic congestion;
   (d)   reduce air pollution, noise and visual intrusion;
   (e)   reduce accidents.
3 Financial and economic
   (a)   maximise revenue;
   (b)   minimise unit cost of operation;
   (c)   preserve flexibility for adjusting fare levels to meet new revenue targets or market demands;
   (d)   ensure efficient use of scarce resources;
   (e)   encourage greater use of spare capacity;
   (f)   conserve energy.
4 Operational
   (a)   maintain access to information about passenger demand;
   (b)   improve efficiency of ticketing and fare collection;
   (c)   facilitate one man bus operation and alleviate staffing difficulties;
   (d)   reduce fare evasion and fraud;
   (e)   maintain incentives to improved management performance.

2.4   Alternative fares policies

In deciding how to meet such objectives a local authority can choose between a variety of options which invariably involve trading off some objectives against others. It is convenient to consider these options in three categories.

The first is concerned with *fare level* – the money values at which fares are charged, which could range from between being entirely free to being set at a level which enables the service to be run at a profit.

The second is concerned with *fare structure* – the way in which fares are paid. The main options are to have either

1   graduated fares, where the charge is related to the distance travelled; or
2   flat fares, under which the same fare is paid no matter what the distance travelled; or
3   zonal fares, under which the city is divided into several zones, with fares at a flat rate for all travel within a designated number of zones and extra charges made for crossing the boundaries.

Each one of these can be introduced in conjunction with differing amounts and styles of prepurchase, usually at a substantial discount, the main methods being:

1 system passes which allow unlimited travel on any vehicle in the system during the period of validity of the ticket;
2 multijourney tickets, sold in books or strips of single tickets each of which can be used once for any journey over the distance for which it is valid; and
3 season tickets, valid for a certain period for any number of journeys between two defined points on the system.

The fare level and structure decided on should take account of the prospects for discriminatory differential pricing — between routes (line pricing) and times of day (peak/off peak pricing), as well as between different modes and services. Thus, for example, peak services could be priced higher than off peak, trains higher than buses, and special bus services like minibus and dial a bus higher than the conventional bus services. Indeed, different pricing structures can in theory be adopted for all categories and subdivisions of the total operation which either provide a different quality of service or cater for a different type of passenger; and such a flexible approach to pricing could make a big contribution to several of the objectives in the financial and economic group (3(a), 3(d), and 3(e)). Some fare structures, however, may be obstacles to the adoption of flexible and discriminatory pricing structures within any one mode or service — a flat fare being the chief example.

As a matter of definition, I consider the policy towards differential pricing to be incorporated in the fare level category. The third category concerns the *special concessions* that can be introduced outside the main fare structure, once the general fare level has been determined in this way. They could, for example, be offered to specific groups of people (such as families travelling together, the elderly and children); and have the effect of improving the attractiveness and availability of the service for such groups by enabling them to pay lower fares than those required by the general fares level. In nearly all circumstances, it has been found that reducing public transport fares does not generate enough extra demand to prevent receipts from falling as well. The special concessions are therefore concerned with how lower than average prices can contribute to social and environmental objectives; whereas the differential pricing policies incorporated in the general fares level are more often concerned with how higher than average prices can improve overall profitability.

Figure 2.1 shows some of the factors affecting the relationship between

24

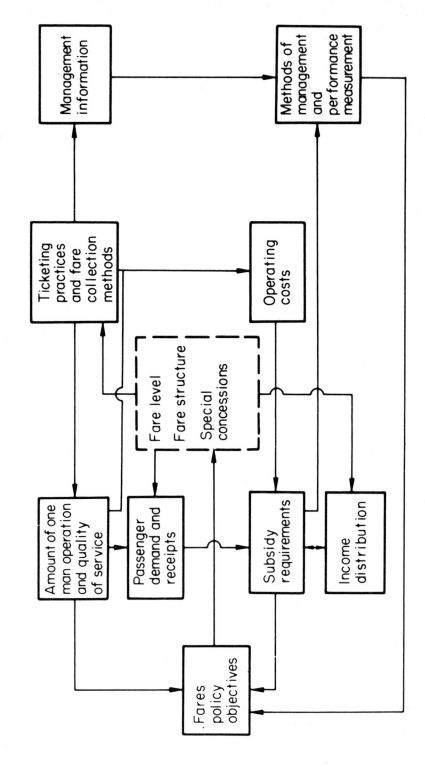

Fig. 2.1   Factors affecting the relationship between alternative fares policies and the objectives they serve

these alternative fares policies and the objectives they serve.[7] Low fare levels, for example, could lead to higher demand but lower receipts, thus calling for subsidy from central or local taxes. Again a bus flat fare could enable improvements to be made in ticketing arrangements to allow faster fare collection, thus making it possible to extend the scope for one man operation and alleviate staffing difficulties. However, in view of the predominance of short distance passengers on most urban bus services, a change from a graduated to a flat fare system would be likely to lead to a sharp drop in either passengers or receipts, according to the level at which it was set.

The box referring to management information relates to the operational objective 4(a). The information gained by public transport operators from tickets is an excellent yardstick against which to assess the use of the service at different times of day, in different areas of the city, by different journey lengths, and in many other ways. And although in many cities this information is neither extracted nor used for these purposes, its availability provides considerable potential for improving both the planning and operation of the public transport services. Moreover, if the information is not available from tickets, it can only be obtained by the less reliable and administratively more complicated and expensive process of mounting special sample surveys.

The amount of information that can be obtained from tickets is constrained by the degree to which fares vary with distance. A finely graduated fare structure will give a large amount but a flat fare considerably less. With free fares all this information is lost, unless free tickets are issued in which case the advantages of reduced operating costs that would otherwise have followed from the policy are lost instead.

2.5   Choosing the right policy

Figure 2.1 does not by itself reveal the conflict between objectives which is the main problem in choosing between different fares policies. Some objectives are likely to be incompatible almost by definition. But even if that does not arise, it is logically impossible to choose a unique policy on the grounds that it gives the best performance in attaining several independent objectives, unless the alternatives being considered all push in the same direction towards achieving them. And this is rarely the case. Free fares, for example, will contribute to some operational objectives (4(b) and 4(c)) but not to others (4(a)). They will help more than any other fares policy with reducing traffic congestion (2(c)), but at the expense of, for example, alleviating overcrowding in the peaks (1(c)). And although they make a strongly adverse contribution to some financial and economic objectives (3(a) particularly), they assist the achievement of others (3(b)).

In this situation the only methods of determining the 'best' policy are:

(a)   to choose just one of the objectives as the most important and treat all the others as constraints; or

(b)   to convert the several objectives into a single one by assuming a predetermined trade off between them; or

(c)   to search for solutions which are satisfactory or good enough (satisficing, in Simon's terminology[8]) rather than optimal.

In the first case it is relatively easy to choose the right policy. For in situations in which policy makers are able to agree that just one of their objectives can be taken as out-weighing all the others, there are a number of well developed optimisation techniques which can be used to discover the best solution to any particular problem. These methods (of which linear programming is perhaps the most widely used example) involve defining a socalled *objective function* which measures the extent to which that dominant objective has been achieved; and the other aims are subordinated as constraints which limit how far you can go in that direction. For example, if maximisation of revenue (3(a)) were taken as the most important objective, the extent to which it could be achieved through higher fare levels might be constrained in some predetermined way so as to prevent too great a loss in passengers and thus too adverse a contribution to objectives such as 1(b) and 2(c). In practice, however, the relative importance that is normally attached to each of the wide range of conflicting objectives which face local government in fares policy makes it impossible to pick out revenue maximisation or any other single goal as the dominant one in that manner. It is very difficult to find a way round this dilemma, which arises in many other management situations as well; and in spite of the enormous amount of research on this subject from several disciplines (economics, sociology, organisation theory, psychology and town planning) no satisfactory solution has yet emerged.

The only comprehensive review of the literature that has yet appeared is dedicated 'to Helle and Peter who achieve many objectives every day without decision models'.[9] This is an important reminder that the information and intuitive judgements used by managers in taking their 'seat of the pants' decisions, can only be improved by the use of analytical tools if they are constructed with the greatest care and rigour as a set of relevant, consistent and testable propositions. The temptation to

26

introduce new subjective judgements masked as science must be strongly resisted.

This temptation arises particularly with the second of the above methods in which the several objectives are converted into a single one, usually by weighting them with numbers whose size indicates their relative importance. For this makes it very difficult to avoid introducing new and untested judgements which will add nothing but confusion to what is already a complicated enough decision problem.

This method of approach has other fundamental drawbacks as well. There is first the fundamental quandary of welfare economics that it is impossible to devise a unique criterion to measure the attainment of social welfare without sacrificing certain basic principles of rationality and democracy. [10] Furthermore, this process involves deriving the weights either by making independent judgements about their magnitude, or from an independent hypothesis about an overriding objective which by implication is assumed to reflect what policy makers consider to be their most important aim in life. [11] Both of these methods of calculating the weights involve ducking a whole series of issues concerned with appreciating the interdependence of objectives, and the need to monitor progress against each one of them individually, taking corrective action where necessary.

A brief review of some of the more popular techniques now in use may help to clarify these remarks. This review is not intended to do full justice to the techniques being considered, and is far from being a full appraisal of the enormous amount of investigation and analysis that has been carried out in this area. Its only purpose is to bring out what seem to be the most critical issues relevant to the management of fares policy.

Cost-benefit analysis, which is heavily used in transport planning, assumes implicitly that policy makers' prime concern is to maximise an objective function defined in terms of the economist's concept of 'consumer surplus'. [12] Variables relevant to the decision problem, apart from money costs and benefits, are converted into equivalent money values by multiplying them by weights derived from that assumption. (Travelling time is the most important variable treated in this way in transport planning.)

This is undoubtedly a useful tool in public sector decision making. For while it tends to bury important factors, it can be conducted so as to expose some of them and can be applied to complex problems in a consistent and rigorous fashion. It is, however, important to recognise the limitations of this technique. The main trouble is that the maximisation of consumer surplus cannot normally be taken as a fair reflection of the policy maker's most important objective. (Other objectives like income distribution may be at least as important.) Moreover, the concept depends on accepting certain highly restrictive assumptions such as that the gain of an extra £1 is worth as much to a rich man as to a poor man. It was, indeed, dismissed by one eminent economist a long time ago as being of 'historical and doctrinal interest with a limited amount of appeal as a purely mathematical puzzle'.[13]

The narrowness of the objectives implicit in the typical cost benefit approach to transport planning and of the parameters used to assess their attainment does not always seem to be sufficiently appreciated — as in a recent study of 'optimal' fares subsidies which naturally (in view of the method adopted) had to conclude that they were zero when roads were uncongested.[14] On the other hand several modifications to cost benefit analysis have been specially developed to meet such criticisms, and are now widely used in British urban planning. The first was Lichfield's 'Planning Balance Sheet',[15] in which all the important costs and benefits arising from a plan are described in tabular form — quantifying them in their original measuring units where possible, otherwise noting them as intangibles. The advantage of this approach is that it deliberately avoids all the pitfalls mentioned above. It was, however, initially little more than a rather complicated presentational device, and provided no constructive analytical solution to the multiobjective decision problem. Some modifications that have since been introduced to meet the latter criticism are discussed below.

Another tool popular with British urban planners is Hill's 'goals achievement matrix'[16] which although intended as an improvement on the Planning Balance Sheet, falls right into the trap of requiring weights to be drawn out of a hat and applied to the several objectives. There is also the technique known as AIDA[17] (Analysis of Inter-connected Decision Areas), which although evolved from many fascinating insights into the theory and practice of planning, is open to the criticism of introducing subjective judgements masked as science, which are no better than the decision makers' intuitive judgements that they are intended to replace.

It is perhaps not surprising that these methods have run into difficulties, since they have been developed . to handle broad, long-term, strategic urban planning issues which inevitably have a high qualitative or even philosophical content. By contrast, if we turn to the last of the three lines of solution mentioned earlier — that of satisficing rather than optimising — the methods of approach have been mainly developed for and applied to sharper, shorter term, and more quantitative business type decision problems. The most promising developments have been in the area of goal programming and related techniques, which are basically extensions of and modifications to linear programming with the specific aim of handling multiobjective decision problems. Their common feature is that all the goals are treated as constraints; and although the methods usually involve some ordering or weighting of goals they are an improvement on the methods previously discussed in that they provide information for managers about the degree to which each one of the goals is attained.

Perhaps the most interesting of these developments is Ijiri's use of goal indicator charts. [18] These charts enable managers, by means of easily observable indicators, to determine at any point in time potential inconsistencies between the organisation's various goals and subgoals and their relation to actual performance. This is an attractive approach in view of the problems faced in the management of fares policy, for it recognises and takes explicit account of the hierarchical nature of both objectives and management structure (a particularly important point in view of the split responsibilities between local government and public transport operators), and also gets right into the heart of the management situation by providing feedback to managers for monitoring performance against objectives.

Further research and practical experiments would have to be under-taken before any precise suggestions could be made as to how any of these approaches could be developed to apply to the management of fares policy. In the meantime, I would suggest a two level approach, based on the principle that a clear separation of responsibilities between the public transport operators and the controlling political authorities makes not only for more efficient day-to-day management but also for more effective policy control. [19]

2.6 Day-to-day management

For the operator, the relatively uniform and comparable nature of his 'product' makes it possible for him to adopt the first of the three lines of solution suggested earlier: namely to choose just one of these goals as the most important, with all the others subordinated as constraints. Moreover, compared with many government programmes, the operator has more immediate control over the activities for which he is responsible, and access to reliable information about the degree to which his chosen objective is being achieved. Thus he is able to choose a straightforward and unambiguous single goal, which can be used to monitor progress and as an incentive to improved performance.

This single goal should also be chosen so as to reflect in some way the political authority's wider social and economic objectives, which means that it must as a minimum be output rather than input oriented. London Transport has already done a great deal of work in preparing and using a simple, unambiguous and output oriented goal of that kind. The single objective they have chosen is maximisation of passenger miles sold. [20] And this was confirmed by the Greater London Council in January 1975 through the issue of a general directive that 'the London Transport Executive shall aim to maximise passenger miles within the level of financial resources decided by the Council subject to any specific stipulations that the Council may make from time to time.' [21] The 'specific stipulations' referred to in the directive are there to ensure that the council is not prevented from requiring the executive to undertake projects to achieve social and strategic objectives even if this should prove inconsistent with the main goal. The GLC's decision in March 1975 to reduce the fares charged on night bus services to normal (they had been double the normal adult fare before then) is an example. The loss in revenue is unlikely to be offset by any increase in passenger miles (night bus passengers are largely a captive market) so could certainly have been spent elsewhere to better effect in terms of passenger miles maximisation. However, the responsible committees in reporting to council commented as follows: 'Many of the passengers who use night buses are workers whose employment requires them to travel at these times, and on social policy grounds we feel that the double fares arrangement should be terminated.' [22]

The only constraint in the directive which relates to London Transport's internal management performance is on outlays from the financial budget, but it would be perfectly possible to extend the approach to bring in other constraints as well. Apart from money, the most critical constraint faced by many public transport operators is staff shortage. In theory at any rate, it would seem desirable to extend London Transport's approach so as to develop an internal management procedure for public transport operators under which projects are chosen so as to maximise their contribution to a single goal such as maximising passenger miles; but with both the money and the numbers of staff in critical grades that are consumed (or saved) by each project costed in a way that reflected their relative scarcity. [23]

2.7   Policy control

The multiple and conflicting objectives faced by the controlling political authorities make it impossible for them to find a crisp management solution on the lines discussed above. Most of the other procedures discussed earlier are either insufficiently developed (goal indicator charts) or have severe analytical drawbacks (cost-benefit analysis, for example). An interesting example is that in the night buses policy decision just referred to, the passenger miles maximisation approach led to a different (but positive) conclusion to that reached by the GLC in its broad social and strategic evaluation. Cost benefit analysis, however, would have been unable to reach any conclusion at all. For a start, there are no time savings to be compared and measured, so that one of the main strengths of cost benefit analysis in transport planning is not relevant to this particular decision problem. Further, being a largely captive market, the price people would have been 'willing to pay' for night buses is either a rather meaningless concept, or else raises wider issues of income distribution that are beyond the scope of cost benefit analysis on its own to handle.

Until further research has been undertaken, the most promising way of helping local governments take their strategic decisions on fares policy would seem to be through developing and modifying Lichfield's Planning Balance Sheet approach. As already noted, the main need is to extend it from being a rather complicated presentational device to give some more positive assistance in making the choice between several alternatives in the face of conflicting objectives. Lichfield himself has extended his original approach so as to incorporate a method of weighting objectives, while recognising the difficulties this involves. In a later published study, a method was used which would 'as far as possible allow the elected representatives to see the results of alternative weightings, either set out by the consultants or worked out for themselves.'[24] This method avoids some (but not all) of the snags discussed earlier in the chapter. However, the procedure still seems to be too complicated, and too dependent for interpretation on highly skilled analysts. Further, it requires the decision makers to have considerable reserves of patience in order to wade through a mass of abstract intellectual arguments before coming to a practical policy conclusion.

Ideally, what we need is a method which is not only at least as successful as Lichfield's in avoiding the analytical pitfalls described earlier, but is at the same time either much simpler, or much more mechanistic, or both. As a start, a simple table could be drawn up to show the relative contribution of alternative fares policies to the objectives that have been chosen. These contributions would show the changes caused by each policy from the previous situation, measured where possible in terms of the quantitative parameter most relevant to the achievement of each chosen objective. Where quantitative measures were not available the

31

alternative policies would be compared just by making judgements about how their relative contributions ranked against each other in order of importance.

The first and most important choice for the local authority in fares policy is over the general level at which the fares should be set. This choice raises a number of other problems which are discussed in detail in the next chapter. But the initial decision ought to be taken bearing in mind factors such as those illustrated in Table 2.3.

Four alternative fare level options are assessed against objectives picked out of the full list described earlier so as to illustrate how the method might work. The figures should be regarded as notional, though they bear some resemblance to reality. They refer to London Transport fares, with the base line being the fare level and structure operating before fares were raised in March 1975. The three fare level options apart from free fares are the same as those discussed in the GLC's consultation paper produced at the end of 1974.[25]

Table 2.3 shows that in moving from a low to a high fare level we gain against some objectives – 1(c), 3(a) – but lose against others – 2(c), 3(e). There is also a once and for all loss against 4(b) in moving away from free fares. This loss can only be reversed by changing to a simpler bus fare structure, such as a flat bus fare, which can be seen by looking at the effect of moving away from the previous finely graduated bus fare structure to the two simpler fare structures that are also shown in the table – again taken from the consultation paper. But once again, the advantages of simpler bus fare structures against objectives such as 4(b) are offset by disadvantages in relation to others. For example, simpler fare structures require higher minimum fare values to bring in the same amount of revenue, thus leading to a greater loss in passengers and an adverse contribution to objectives like 3(e).

The full table will, of course, be more complicated, since it would normally be necessary to consider a wider range of objectives than the six picked out here. However, even with the full list of twenty one objectives suggested earlier, the table would still be a straightforward and clear summary of the pros and cons of various courses of action. But there are still two problems to be overcome before using it as a regular decision making tool. There is first the quality of the information contained in the table. This depends critically on an ability to make reliable estimates of the effects of fares changes, and some of the later chapters discuss the difficulties this involves. Nevertheless, for those local authorities and operators who would be unable initially to produce very many reliable quantitative estimates, the table could be completed with ordinal rather

Table 2.3

Illustrative effects of alternative fares policies on selected objectives

Objectives	Measuring units	Alternative fare levels				Alternative bus fare structures (pence)		
		free (1)	base levels (2)	+30% (3)	+45% (4)	3-5-8-10 13-15-18-20 (5)	4-8-12 (6)	6 (7)
1 Social 1(c) Peak overcrowding	% reduction in peak passenger miles sold	−30	−1	+5	+7	0	+1	+2
2 Environmental 2(c) Traffic congestion	% reduction in peak traffic flows	+10	+0.5	−1	−1.5	0	0	0
3 Financial and economic 3(a) Revenue	% gain in revenue	−100	+1	+24	+36	0	0	0
3(e) Spare capacity	% gain in off peak passenger miles sold	+60	+2	−10	−15	0	−1	−2
4 Operational 4(a) Information access	ordinal	−3	0	0	0	0	−1	−2
4(b) Ticketing and fare collection	reduction in marginal boarding times on one-man buses (seconds per passenger)	+2.8	0	0	0	0	+1.5	+2.0

(1) The alternative fare levels assume no change in the base structure shown in column (5).
(2) The alternative bus fare structures are designed to maintain the base revenue. However, the bus flat fare of 6p assumes that there would be no diversion from the underground to take advantage of the much cheaper bus fare for longer distances. If this did happen, there could be excessive overcrowding on buses and some operating difficulties, unless either underground fares were reduced or the bus flat fare were increased.

than cardinal rankings which would still give a better basis for decision making than doing nothing.

The second problem brings us back to what has been the main issue discussed in this chapter: how, if at all, can more positive guidance be given to help the policy makers actually come to a decision. Remember not only that the objectives are incompatible, but that no two members of the average local government transport committee (or of any other group meeting to take a decision) will rank them all in precisely the same order of importance. Thus it is not possible to press a button and hope that the 'right' answer will emerge automatically. In fact there can be no such thing as a single correct solution unless this is defined by some higher law (such as an imposed weighting of objectives) under which the committee members' individual preferences are submerged. Otherwise the decision has to be a compromise between conflicting preferences.

But although the decision has in the end to incorporate the subjective judgements of those responsible for making it, the foundations on which it is built must be as objective and reliable as possible. In other words, the aim should be to ensure that the decision makers are provided with as much information relevant to the decision as they can handle, with the basic data analysed in a way that rigorously observes the rules of logic and scientific method.

A table on the lines suggested above could be a first step in that process. Perhaps the next should be to explore whether a systematic analysis could be undertaken so as to reveal to the decision makers each other's relative preferences for alternative policies and objectives. This could range from a simple voting procedure, to a much more sophisticated analysis based on the methods used in psychometrics and other disciplines to study consumer preferences. [26] (The latter type of analysis might be able to indicate not only policy makers' preferences for different objectives and policy options, but also the consistency between them, and even how they related to party political positions and other individual characteristics.) This would provide a new body of information to assist the decision, over and above the facts and figures collected in the table. An approach on these lines, which lays the stress on deliberately searching for relevant information while respecting the decision makers' right and duty to make their own subjective choice in the end, is surely to be preferred to the other methods which allow the analysts themselves to distort the decision process with their own subjective judgements.

But this is only half the story. For the local authority must not only introduce a suitable procedure for choosing between alternative fares policies. It must also work out a clear framework of groundrules so that decisions are taken, and programmes implemented, in a way that ensures that all the operators' day-to-day management actions (those that affect quality of service directly as well as those which carry out the chosen fares policy) contribute to the local council's objectives. That broad issue is covered in the next chapter.

Notes

[1] Transport Act 1968, section 20.

[2] Transport (London) Act 1969, section 28.

[3] For a fuller definition of corporate planning see A. Grey, *Organising for Corporate Planning*, Local Government Studies, October 1972.

[4] R. Townsend, *Up the Organisation*, Coronet Books, 1971.

[5] Local Government Act 1974, section 6(5).

[6] This is a development of some ideas first expressed in A. Grey, *The Role of Local Government in Fares Policy*, Transport and Road Research Laboratory Supplementary Report 37UC, 1974.

[7] Figure 2.1 is developed from D.A. Quarmby's in *Effect of Alternative Fares Systems on Operational Efficiency: British Experience*, Transport and Road Research Laboratory Supplementary Report 37UC, 1974.

[8] See, for example, H.A. Simon, 'Theories of Decision-Making in Economics and Behavioural Science', *American Economic Review*, June 1959.

[9] E. Johnsen, *Studies in Multiobjective Decision Models*, Studentlitteratur, 1968.

[10] K.J. Arrow, *Social Choice and Individual Values*, John Wiley, 1953.

[11] In this latter case the weights can be derived as 'shadow prices' which are found as the solution to the dual of the linear programming problem; provided the objective function defining achievement against the principal objective, and the constraints which affect the other objectives, are all linear.

[12] This concept refers to the benefits obtained by consumers through charging them less than the maximum they would have been willing to pay for the commodity in question. It is measured by the amount of extra revenue that could in theory have been obtained (which is the same as the size of the area on the demand curve above the price line).

[13] P.A. Samuelson, *Foundations of Economic Analysis*, Harvard, 1948.

[14] R. Jackson, 'Optimal Subsidies for Public Transit', *Journal of Transport Economics and Policy*, January 1975, p. 8.

[15] N. Lichfield, 'Cost-benefit Analysis in City Planning', *Journal of the American Institute of Planners,* November 1960.

[16] M. Hill, 'A Goals Achievement Matrix for Evaluating Alternative Plans', *Journal of the American Institute of Planners,* January 1968.

[17] J.K. Friend, and N. Jessop, *Local Government and Strategic Choice,* Tavistock, 1969.

[18] Y. Ijiri, *Management Goals and Accounting for Control,* North Holland, 1965.

[19] For a detailed justification of this principle, including the specification of criteria for deciding what kind of public sector activities should be managed separately by autonomous boards, see A. Grey and A. Simon, 'People, Structure and Civil Service Reform', *Journal of Management Studies,* October 1970.

[20] For a clear justification of this as a suitable single goal for public transport operators, see E.R. Ellen and I. Phillips, 'Resource Allocation in the Non-Profit Maximising Situation', *UITP Review,* 1975.

[21] Greater London Council Minutes 1975, p. 68.

[22] Greater London Council Minutes 1974, p. 568.

[23] This could, for example, by done by multiplying outlays from the financial budget, and staff numbers, by shadow prices derived from a linear programming procedure.

[24] N. Lichfield and H. Chapman, 'Cost Benefit Analysis and Road Proposals for a Shopping Centre', *Journal of Transport Economics and Policy,* September 1968.

[25] *Fare Deal – Your Choice,* GLC, 1974.

[26] See, for example, R. Dobson, T.F. Golob, R.L. Gustafson, 'Multidimensional Scaling of Consumer Preferences for a Public Transportation System', *Socio-Economic Planning Sciences,* February 1974.

3 The Control of Fare Levels

The problems discussed in the last chapter are common to many different management situations. But in one aspect of fares policy – the control of fare levels – there are extra and much more unusual difficulties to be surmounted. This chapter discusses the nature of these additional problems and considers how they might be resolved, concentrating once again on the British experience.

3.1 Background

The bus is the predominant form of urban passenger transport in Britain. The railways, by contrast, cater primarily for comparatively long distance travel between towns; and as we have seen, London is the only town where there is a substantial amount of travel by suburban railway services.

Britain's national railway services went through a severe financial and economic crisis in the early 1960s. In 1963 the British Railways Board published some radical proposals to deal with the crisis, which included massive cuts in those services judged by the board to be unable to earn sufficient revenue to cover their direct operating costs. Some 290 passenger services were to be completely withdrawn, and 2,360 stations and 5,000 route miles to be closed, accounting for something like a third of the total railway network.[1] Although this led to a large number of closures actually being put into effect, many stations and services survived: partly because of strong local opposition to the closures and partly because of the emergence of a new political philosophy that special payments out of public funds should be made to support services judged desirable on social grounds but unable to pay their way commercially.

Until recently, urban public transport in the United Kingdom has managed to escape a major crisis of that kind. Both the bus and suburban railway services succeeded in covering their costs by a combination of regular increases in fares and modest injections of subsidy, mainly on the capital side. The responsible government bodies were able to let events almost take care of themselves, and virtually opt out of taking decisions on fare levels which went through as a matter of course. For the bus industry, however, the continuing increase in fare levels has helped to reinforce a long and continuing erosion of demand and service levels, as illustrated in Table 3.1. The largest volume of passengers carried on all forms of public road transport (not only buses and coaches, but also trolley buses and trams which have now been virtually phased out) was in 1950. By 1973 the passenger journeys had halved but receipts had nearly trebled — representing more than a fivefold increase in average fare per journey. This also meant that increases in fares kept well ahead of the growth in the general price level caused by inflation. The table also shows that the average fare per journey nearly doubled between 1950 and 1973 even when the figures are converted to 1950 money values.

Table 3.1

Public road transport in Great Britain: passenger journeys and receipts

	Passenger journeys (million)	Passenger receipts (£ million)	Average fare per passenger journey (pence)	
			actual prices	constant (1950) prices*
1950	16,706	208·35	1·25	1·25
1960	13,680	314·73	2·30	1·55
1970	9,154	448·08	4·89	2·17
1973	8,455	580·71	6·87	2·39

Source: *Passenger Transport in Great Britain* 1971, (Table 30) and 1973 (Table 41).

*Actual prices deflated by retail price index.

Moreover, several events have now coalesced to bring about a more severe crisis for urban public transport than that which beset the national railways in the early 1960s. The energy crisis which developed in 1974 triggered off the worst economic recession that Britain (along with most industrialised countries) had faced for forty years, against a background of accelerating inflation, rising unemployment, and increasing urban strife. In addition, large numbers of people are dependent on the bus as their only form of transport, with no practical alternative but to stop travelling if their bus is taken away or priced out of their reach. And for those who do have a car available for their journey, their decision to go by car instead often adds to traffic congestion and associated environmental ills.

3.2   A triangular choice

These acute and wideranging problems make it even more important for
fare levels to be determined as a result of careful consideration by the
local authority of all the relevant objectives. Moreover, decisions on fare
levels should also be taken as part of a triangular choice between raising
fares, and the two other main methods of finding (or saving) the extra
money needed to pay for the rapidly escalating costs – increasing
subsidies from public funds, and cutting services. The choice should
depend on the total impact on objectives of alternative ways of drawing
the whole triangle, not just the fare level vertex. But, as we have seen,
decisions on fare levels in British towns have had their own indefatigable
momentum, with no deliberate consideration given to subsidy or service
level alternatives – though lower service levels has been one of the
inevitable consequences of that process. Only for the national railways has
a conscious decision been taken in favour of an alternative to higher fares,
namely the service cuts following the 1963 reshaping proposals. Moreover,
the triangular choice problem is now being avoided by a tendency to turn
the argument round so as to imply that there is only a choice between one
of two extremes: what I have described elsewhere as the nationalised
industry and welfare state approaches to public expenditure.[2]

The former approach is summed up as follows in a White Paper giving
guidelines as to how the nationalised industries should be run. 'The aim of
pricing policy should be that the consumer should pay the true costs of
providing the goods and services he consumes, in every case where these
can be sensibly identified.'[3] Exceptions are, however, made for special
payments out of public funds aimed at supporting unremunerative services
judged desirable on social grounds, or at helping identified groups of
people in need. By contrast the welfare state approach asserts that certain
social services should be taken out of the market place and provided to
everybody either free or at a heavily subsidised price, thus making the
state collectively responsible for ensuring that a certain minimum level of
provision is available to all people regardless of individual circumstances.

There are sound arguments in favour of either of these two alternatives.
For the nationalised industry approach, which has until recently dominated thinking about the management of the British public transport
industry, it is argued that rationing by the price mechanism is the fairest
way of allocating resources and avoids market distortions; while special
separate provision for identified people in need is the best way of making
sure that help goes to where it is most required. For the welfare state
approach, it is argued that it is impossible to identify effectively those in

need, quite apart from the social stigma attached to such identification; and the cumbersome administrative machinery that would be needed for better identification would defeat its own purpose. Furthermore, it is maintained that this approach provides the opportunity to take positive action to change the whole pattern of resource allocation, so as to achieve broader social and economic objectives in the public interest.

There are, however, an infinite number of choices on fare levels between making sure that public transport pays its way (or is even run at a profit) out of income from fares charged to passengers, and treating it as a free social service. Although neither of these two extremes is necessarily wrong, any local authority, whatever its political complexion, could find that a choice somewhere in between fitted in better with its own chosen objectives.

Periods of economic crisis and high inflation should not be allowed to divert attention from the need to choose from a wider range of alternatives. Indeed, a harrowing external environment highlights the importance of making the right decision as a result of considering a wide range of choices in relation to carefully chosen objectives. Some of the points to be borne in mind while taking this decision are discussed further below, considering each side of the triangle in turn.

3.3 Fare and service levels

In considering the various choices between fare and service levels, it is necessary to get behind the travel experience on which the policy objectives listed in the last chapter were based. For people rarely travel just for the sake of it. They need to move around for a variety of purposes such as earning money, visiting friends, going to school and getting to the doctor. These final aims can be obtained only at a price, which includes the cost of using up time and of physical effort and inconvenience, as well as direct money costs.

Both types of cost can be changed by policy decisions. Fares policy is, of course, the main influence on money costs. Time and effort costs would be tackled primarily through service improvements such as building new roads and railways, different methods of traffic management, and changes in the type and style of operation of public transport services. But fares policy can also affect 'time and effort' costs indirectly by, for example, reducing road congestion and improving the efficiency of ticketing and fare collection (i.e. by contributing to objectives 2(c) and 4(b) in the suggested list).

40

It is a widely held view that it is 'better' to spend money on service improvements than on fare subsidies. The two different lines of argument that are commonly put forward in support of that view are discussed below.

The first is that people in general prefer to get there quicker than to pay less for the journey: or to put it another way, the time and effort costs of the journey are more onerous to them than the money costs. There is some limited evidence in support of that assertion, both from market research surveys, and from studies which attempt to measure directly the response of passengers to service level as well as fare changes.[4] But not all of this evidence tells the same story which is hardly surprising since the same dilemma arises here as with the earlier discussion of decision makers' policy preferences. Not all individuals will rank the relative importance to them of the money and time and effort costs of their journeys in the same order of importance. Poor people, for example, are likely to be more anxious about high fares than service quality, whereas the preferences of rich people might be the other way round. And since policy makers are bound to be concerned with differences of this kind rather than with the preference of the 'average' passenger, if he exists, the policy decision is by no means clearcut. What may be needed once again is the development and use of methods of studying consumers' preferences in relation to their social and economic characteristics. In fact the study of consumer preferences referred to earlier did attempt to do this.[5] Using the appropriate statistical techniques, consumers' preferences for a wide range of attributes of a public transport service were compared with their social and economic characteristics. Among other things, this method of analysis showed that older people and individuals from large families placed considerable importance on a low fare; whereas that factor was of little concern to rich or highly educated people, who tended to put various quality of service characteristics first. Similar conclusions can also be drawn from studies which have shown that people value time savings relatively more highly than money savings as their income increases.[6] A final objection to the bland statement that people prefer service improvements to fares concessions is that their preferences depend on the situation they are faced with, as well as on who they are. Thus when the service is good but fares are high, passengers will naturally tend to consider fares reductions as a more important priority than further service improvements.

The second line of argument is that service improvements are more cost effective in meeting defined aims than fares subsidies. What has so far been the most comprehensive exposition of that view formed part of a detailed analysis of the effects of free fares in the city of Boston (in the United States) carried out in 1967 by Charles Rivers Associates.[7] They considered how effective free fares on the one hand, and direct service improvements on the other, would be in contributing to three defined aims. Although these aims were stated in a different form in the study, they are of a similar type to the following three objectives taken out of the list on pp. 21–2.

1   Improve travel opportunities for disadvantaged groups (1(b)).
2   Encourage movement to strategic centres (2(b)).
3   Reduce traffic congestion (2(c)).

The total cost of changing to a free fare system in Boston was estimated at $75·3 million per year: accounted for by adding the full operating and capital costs of the existing services ($70·4 million) to the equivalent costs for the extra services that would be needed to cope with the additional demand ($8·4 million); and subtracting the savings in fare collection costs ($3·5 million). By comparison, the following could be achieved in relation to the three objectives by providing special services:

1   At an annual cost of $4·3 million (or 6 per cent of the cost of free fares) job opportunities for poor people could be improved by providing a special, high frequency bus service running between all the low income residential areas and low skilled employment centres in Boston.
2   At an annual cost of $12·0 million (or one sixth of the cost of free fares) sufficient improvements could be obtained in the quality of the existing bus services to generate about half the stimulus to shopping trips to strategic centres that would have been provided by free fares.
3   The same service improvements would reduce car traffic by 6 per cent in the morning peak and 4 per cent in the evening peak, compared with corresponding figures for the impact of free fares of 9 per cent and 6 per cent respectively. In other words, service improvements at one sixth of the cost of free fares would reduce traffic congestion in the rush hours by two thirds as much.

On the other hand, three separate theoretical studies undertaken for London were all more optimistic in their estimates of the benefits to be derived from free fares. The first compared the travel behaviour of London Transport employees who have free use of buses and tubes and pay only 25 per cent of British Rail fares, with other central London employees paying the normal prices; and estimated that if these concessions were generally available car commuting to central London might be cut by as much as two thirds.[8] The other two studies were undertaken by the Transport and Road Research Laboratory and used computer models to estimate directly the effects of free fares policies.[9] One of their conclusions was that blanket free fares in inner London (roughly the old London County Council area) would yield substantial benefits to travellers as a result of free travel, reduced congestion and newly generated trips. If the costs of laying on additional services and losses in revenue to operators and in taxes to government were all subtracted, these benefits would still amount to a sum equivalent to nearly one half of total operating costs.

A further point is that in many towns the marginal costs of service improvements may be much higher than those estimated by Charles Rivers Associates, in view of the current shortage of staff in the public service industries, which may well continue even in periods of economic recession. Public transport operators are often forced into the position of paying premium rates to attract the staff necessary to prevent the service from declining, let alone effect any improvements. And because of the higher wages that now have to be paid to public transport operating staff in many cities, it is likely that for any given sum spent on improving the service, a far greater number of passenger miles could be generated for an equivalent loss in fares revenue (resulting either from an actual reduction in fares, or from raising them by a lower amount than otherwise).

But the most fundamental objection to the conclusions drawn from the Boston study is that when comparisons are made between money spent on service improvements on the one hand and fares concessions on the other, it should be appreciated that we are not comparing like with like. The main concern of decisions on service changes is with finding the best way of allocating additional real resources so as to create new or improved transport services. Fares subsidies, by contrast, are simply transfer payments from one person's pocket (the taxpayer's) to another's (the public transport passenger's). They do not by themselves exert any direct claim on real resources, provided, of course, that the responsible government bodies ensure that the payments really are transferred. This means that the deficits must be financed out of actual increases in tax levels and not by printing more bank notes. If this is done the only pressure on resources arises indirectly from any different pattern of consumption that might follow. For example, if these transfers of income tended on average to be from rich to poor people, this might lead to increased pressure on real resources resulting from the fact that poor people would be likely to spend most of this extra income, whereas beforehand much of it would have been saved by the rich people from whom it was transferred. As far as public transport planning is concerned, the new claims on resources would result from any new investments that might be required to meet the additional public transport demand generated by the lower fares; though to work out the total indirect impact on real resources, any offsetting reductions in demand for other goods and services caused by the higher taxes would have to be subtracted. The effect of any switch (in either direction) between savings and consumption would also have to be taken into account. In the Boston study the gross extra real resource costs of free fares, without allowing for any offsetting reductions or changes in the mix between savings and consumption, were estimated at $4·9 million ($8·4 million for the required extra capacity, less $3·5 million for the fare collection savings); whereas the real resource costs of the alternative of improving the quality of existing bus services were estimated to be nearly two and a half times greater ($12·0 million).

For these reasons fares policy must be more concerned with how fares changes affect the distribution of existing services between different groups of people, than with the typical investment planning decision of finding the best way of allocating additional real resources at the margin. Choosing the right balance between service improvements and alternative fares options is, of course, a prime requirement in determining an effective set of transport policies. But that choice should be governed by a judgement as to which combination of policies is likely to have the best effect on achieving chosen objectives. It should not be constrained by the erroneous assumption that both service improvements and fares subsidies are fighting for limited funds out of the same bag of coins — a point which brings us conveniently on to the next side of the triangle.

3.4   Fare and subsidy levels

Strangely, the Keynesian stress on the need to be concerned much more with the claims on real resources of alternative policies, than with where the money is to come from to pay for the chosen programmes of action, still does not seem to have penetrated discussions about fares policy. For it is not always appreciated that for any given fare level, only the public transport operator has to treat the total sum of money available to him in his budget as an overriding constraint. By contrast, any government body which has the power to raise taxes can make its pot of gold as big as it likes, apart from the constraints caused by public opinion, pressure on resources, and the extent to which it believes that further increases in taxation will contribute more effectively to its social and economic objectives.

For central government these constraints are fairly severe, as they include not only the normal political problems associated with higher taxation, but also the need to ensure that the economy is 'tuned' in such a way that the most efficient balance is struck between consumption, investment, exports, imports, and so on, in the light of the government's overall aims (on unemployment levels, and the growth and distribution of real income, for example). Local government, however, is in the fortunate position of not being responsible for the effects of local fiscal policies on the balance of payments, or for other factors concerned with the management of the national economy. The local area will also be shielded from the effects of any corrective action that central government might have to take, since such actions would normally have to be applied to the country as a whole.

This does not, of course, mean that local government should selfishly and blindly pursue policies that are against the national interest. Indeed, a policy of high subsidy to public transport from local taxation could contribute positively to some national aims (e.g. on energy conservation) even if it detracted from others. Moreover, greater clarity about the distinct and separate responsibilities of central and local government could lead to more coherent and effective policies at both national and local level. Thus a clear recognition by local government that the wider issues of economic management were outside its responsibility, could help to concentrate the mind on the effects on the local community of the transfers of money that would result from paying for a given public transport service level out of taxes instead of fares. It would also put strong pressure on central government to arrange for the development of more progressive systems of local taxation, and to design other policies which ensured that its own responsibilities for national income distribution (both between regions and between individuals) were more adequately fulfilled.

These transfers of income between the passenger and taxpayer can have a powerful influence on the local council's objectives for the distribution of income within the local community. Chapter 6 explores in some detail the effects on income distribution of switching from a high fare policy to a low fare policy financed from British local property taxes (rates). The main trouble here is that local taxes on property have a more adverse effect on income distribution than the central government taxes on income, which are deliberately designed to tax the rich proportionately more than the poor. This means that if a local authority wished to implement a fares policy based on a high subsidy level, its contribution to the council's income distribution objectives would be enhanced if central government could be persuaded to make a contribution. However, the mix between fare and subsidy levels should be determined as a result of careful consideration of the effects of various policies not just on income distribution, but on the full range of the objectives that have been chosen for fares policy.

3.5   Subsidy and service levels

Having fixed the length and position of two sides of a triangle we do not need Euclid to tell us that the third is also fixed. In other words, having chosen the balance between fare and service levels, and fare and subsidy levels, there is no longer a choice between subsidy and service levels. It is, however, convenient to summarise here the conclusions that seem to be emerging from the above discussion.

The main conclusion is that the local council should choose that combination of fare, subsidy and service levels which between them seem to make the best contribution to its objectives; taking account among other things of the effects on income distribution when deciding how to finance a given service level from fares and subsidy. It must also be remembered that unless services are reduced to match the decline in demand, higher fares will lead to better (i.e. less overcrowded) services, though for the more select group of richer people who can afford to pay for them. Correspondingly unless services are expanded to meet the increased demand, lower fares will lead to a drop in the level of service, though more people will have access to it.

3.6   Coping with inflation

The final major issue to be resolved is the effect of inflation on the triangle. If the operator's costs of providing services were barely changing, the local council could get away with preserving the *status quo* by taking no action on either fare, subsidy or service levels. However, with costs rising as a result of inflation, the council is forced to make a positive choice each year about how the extra costs are to be met. The challenge facing local government is to find a way of taking such decisions so that regular control is maintained over fare and subsidy levels, without either eroding incentives to better performance by the operator, or conflicting with the local authority's wider social and economic objectives.

The main problem is that the higher the rate of wage and price inflation, the more the growth in costs will be dominated by these external influences; and the less will be the influence of changes to the level of service or improvements in productivity and efficiency.

Since costs must always be equal to fares income and subsidy added together, this uncontrollable growth in costs (which will be an important factor even at fairly low rates of inflation) has three important consequences. Firstly, either fares, or subsidy, or both, will also grow at a similar rate determined by influences outside the local council's or the operator's control. Secondly, the only method available to the council for exerting regular and continuing control over either fares or subsidy is to determine that they should rise at a rate related to the independently determined rise' in costs. For otherwise a fresh *ad hoc* decision would have to be taken each year, inevitably resulting in an annual round of unproductive political disputes which would be unlikely to prevent, indeed might positively create, wild and uncomfortable swings in the amounts by which fares or subsidies are increased each year. Further, the consequences of these decisions could not be planned for in advance or related to the forward planning decisions that would need to be taken in other areas of transport policy. Thirdly, the choice open to the council is between controlling either fares or subsidy: both cannot be controlled at the same time.

To see how a system of regular control would work, the two choices indicated by the third point are considered separately below.

3.6.1 *Control over subsidy*

The simplest control over subsidy would be to determine that it rises at a constant multiple n of the growth in costs. In other words if costs were to grow at a compound rate r, the control would be to ensure that subsidy grew at a rate of nr.

Apart from fixing the subsidy at a constant sum ($n = 0$), or gradually extinguishing it ($n < 0$), three different situations could arise with this rule:

1 $n = 1$, reflecting a decision that subsidy should grow at the same rate as costs, which implies that fares income grows at this rate as well, and that the ratio of subsidy (and fares income) to total costs stays constant;

2 $0 < n < 1$, implying that although subsidies are growing, they do so at a slower rate, and fares at a faster rate, than costs. Fares income thus accounts for a higher and higher proportion of costs, though a self financing position is never reached; and

3 $n > 1$, being the converse of $0 < n < 1$. Subsidies will become a higher

and higher proportion of costs, and fares grow at a slower and slower rate until they start falling instead of rising.

Perhaps the two most interesting points associated with this latter option ($n > 1$) are how long it takes first before fares start to fall and secondly before they become free. Clearly this will depend on the size of the cost growth rate and subsidy multiplier, as well as on how great a proportion of total costs is initially paid for through subsidy. To illustrate, assume that the local council is starting from a situation in which it pays subsidy accounting for 10 per cent of costs, and that costs are inflating at a constant rate of 20 per cent per annum. [10] Then the appendix to this chapter shows that the period before fares start decreasing ranges from three years when the subsidy multiplier n is equal to 3 (i.e. the subsidy grows by 60 per cent per annum) to forty-six years when $n = 1\frac{1}{4}$; and that fares become free after periods ranging from six years when $n = 3$ to fifty years when $n = 1\frac{1}{4}$.

3.6.2 *Control over fares*

Once again the simplest control over fares would be to determine that fares income rises at a constant multiple m of the growth in costs. Three parallel situations arise to those discussed for subsidy control. The calculations in the appendix to this chapter are for growth in fares income. Actual fares charged would normally have to grow at a faster rate because of the likely decline in demand following a fares increase.

1   $m = 1$: as with the subsidy rule $n = 1$, this reflects a decision that fares income, costs, and subsidies, should all grow at the same rate.

2   $m > 1$: this is a similar situation to the subsidy rule $0 < n < 1$ but with the important difference that the operator would soon be back to a self financing situation with no subsidies from public funds.

3   $0 < m < 1$: this is similar to the third subsidy rule ($n > 1$) but with the important difference that fares continue to grow, though at a slower rate than costs. Subsidies grow at a faster rate and account for a higher and higher proportion of total costs.

Assuming once again a constant compound cost inflation rate of 20 per cent per annum and subsidies initially at one tenth of total costs, the appendix to this chapter shows that with fares multipliers ranging from between a quarter and three quarters, subsidies will have grown to a quarter of total costs after between one and four years, and to three quarters after between nine and twenty-eight years.

All this is shown in a different way in Figures 3.1 and 3.2, which illustrate how costs, fares income, and subsidies relate to each other when the subsidy multiplier n is greater than one (Fig. 3.1), and when the fares multiplier m is less than one (Fig. 3.2). X and Y on Fig. 3.1 are, of course, the points where fares start to fall and become free and Z is the point at which fares income and subsidy level are equal.

Fig. 3.1   Effect of subsidy control,   Fig. 3.2   Effect of fares control,
$n > 1$ $m < 1$

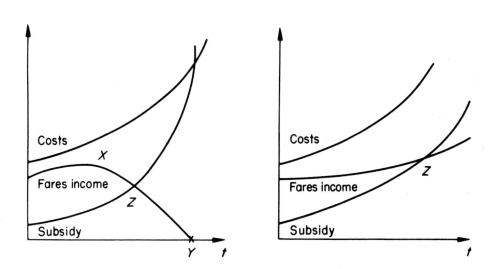

3.7   An index linked subsidy mechanism

To summarise the above discussion, local councils can only exert simple, effective, regular and continuing controls over fares or subsidy if this is done through an index linked mechanism which:

(a)   results in a return to a self financing situation, or at least to a situation in which fares cover a very high proportion of costs; or

(b)   ensures that fares income and subsidy both grow at the same rate as costs, so that subsidy remains at a constant proportion of costs; or

(c)   allows subsidy to grow at a faster rate, or fares at a slower rate, than costs.

Although the last possibility (which is the one illustrated in Figures 3.1 and 3.2) might well be preferred by the majority of local authorities at the present time, the above calculations have revealed the interesting though awkward point that it might well lead eventually to policy implications for the uncontrolled variable which most local councils would not wish to pursue — either free fares if subsidy were controlled, or subsidies accounting for a very high proportion of total costs if fares were controlled.

Whichever control method is used, it is necessary to choose an external index to which the rise in public transport costs, and hence the growth in either fare or subsidy level, can be related. Because the public transport industry is highly labour intensive, the index available from British statistics which is likely to correspond most closely to public transport costs is that for the average earnings of all employees in transport and communications.

There are several reasons why the subsidy level, rather than the fare level, should be controlled in relation to the growth in that external index. In the first place, the subsidy control procedure would enable the local authority to maintain direct control over the raising and issuing of the money to be paid out in subsidy; and leave the operator to decide how fares should be raised to fill the gap between costs and subsidy in association with his own responsibilities for marketing, ticket issuing, fare collection, and so on. If the council were to exercise direct controls over the fare level instead, these management responsibilities would be inverted and thereby confused. Secondly, council control over the subsidy level would give the operator an extra incentive (over and above that provided by the passenger miles maximisation yardstick) to improve his efficiency so as to make his costs rise at a slower rate than the index to which the subsidy was related; thereby enabling him to take the credit for raising fares by a lower amount than would otherwise have been necessary. This important additional incentive would be missing if the council controlled the fare level directly. Finally, the subsidy to be paid out under the subsidy control method could be budgeted for in advance on the basis of forecast changes in the external index, but paid out and accounted for on the basis of the actual changes reported by the Department of Employment which are recorded in the *Monthly Digest of Statistics.* This kind of flexibility and control would not be available with the fare increase decisions required under the fare control method.

So far, however, the only index linked procedure to have been tried out in British local government is the Greater Manchester Council's policy to restrict increases in bus fares to a level in line with the cost of living. This is similar to the fare control method discussed above except that the chosen index is related to the cost of living (the retail price index) rather than the transport industry's costs. But the two methods are virtually indistinguishable provided the cost of living index maintains broadly the same relative relationship to the overall cost index. Thus from 1970–73, for example, the retail price index rose on average by 9 per cent per annum (compound), compared with 12 per cent for the transport and communications earnings index;[11] and if these relative growth rates were maintained, they would imply that the Greater Manchester Council was using, in my terminology, a fares multiplier of three quarters.

Another procedure which has been widely canvassed involves relating the subsidy not to an external index, but to the output produced by the operator. Subsidy could, for example, be paid as a fixed proportion of the number of passenger miles carried above a predetermined threshold or baseline: and would thereby, it is argued, give the operator an incentive to improve the service he provides for the passenger.[12] However, in order to maximise passenger miles for a given subsidy level, the operator would in any case have the incentive to undertake all projects that would cost less in pence per passenger mile generated than could be won back for each passenger mile lost as a result of a fare increase. Hence the threshold subsidy payment would have to be set at a high level to influence the operator's decisions at the margin; and this would have large and unpredictable effects, perhaps out of line with the local authority's wider social and economic objectives. Moreover, these difficulties of encouraging and controlling improvements in performance above the baseline would be enhanced by an even more fundamental dilemma – the fact that the baseline itself is liable to change regardless of the operator's performance. These outside influences could include windfalls like a sharp rise in petrol prices, which might ease traffic congestion and encourage car drivers to divert to public transport, yet have a comparatively small influence on the costs of the labour intensive public transport industry. Or there might be disasters such as strikes or prolonged shortages of spare parts. At the end of the year the independent influence of the operator's own performance in increasing the number of passenger miles carried would be virtually impossible to disentangle. Thus this approach has even more disadvantages than the fare control procedure.

Hence the subsidy control method is the one to go for. In practice this proposal might work out on the following lines. The local authority would first choose its subsidy multiplier – the proportion of the increase in the transport and communications earnings index by which the subsidy is allowed to grow – in the light of a careful consideration of the impact on objectives of different arrangements of the fare-service-subsidy level triangle.

When the budget for the following year was drawn up, it would incorporate on the one hand a provision for subsidy calculated by applying the chosen multiplier to the best available forecast of the growth in the index, and on the other a provision for whatever increase in the fare level was judged necessary by the operator to fill the gap between costs and subsidy in the budget year. Subsidy payments by the council to the operator during the year would be based on the actual changes in the index reported each month by the Department of Employment. Thus if the index rose at a faster rate than forecast, the subsidy would be automatically increased. However, the operator would also have to implement a supplementary increase in fare levels during the year, the amount depending on the extent to which he can prevent his costs from rising as fast as the index. In the reverse situation, with the index rising at a slower rate than forecast, the subsidy would be automatically reduced. But since the new fare level would by then have been implemented, the operator's total income for the budget year would exceed his costs. The obvious solution would be to carry this 'profit' forward, thus enabling a lower fare increase to be implemented in the following year.

For medium term planning, the subsidy multiplier could be fixed at a constant rate for, say, a five year period, and reviewed when the budget and five year plan were rolled forward each year. This would enable the council to escape from the dilemma noted earlier – that if the subsidy multiplier were fixed at a constant greater than one, this would in due course lead to a situation in which fares became free. More generally, the choice of any subsidy multiplier other than one means that it has been decided that the amount of subsidy should grow or decline in real terms at a rate dependent on a wholly arbitrary and uncontrollable index, which again reinforces the need for regular review. (If the multiplier were fixed at one, however, this would reflect a decision to keep the amount of subsidy constant in real terms, whatever the rate of inflation.)

3.8   Changes in service level and fare structure

This index linked subsidy control procedure is concerned with only two sides of the triangle: how to regulate and control the income to be raised from fares and subsidies in an inflationary situation in order to finance and maintain just one chosen level of service. Hence the local council should also be considering at each annual review whether changes in service level were desirable; for example, whether they should be improved to take account of strategic objectives or to accommodate the extra demand resulting from a low fare policy, or reduced to reflect the decline in demand caused by a high fare policy.

It should also be noted that the freedom granted to the operator to change fare levels is not intended to apply to fundamental changes in fare structure or to the introduction of new special concessions, since these can raise wider policy issues not allowed for in the setting of the overall framework. It might be possible to allow for some limited structure changes within that framework by giving the operator special additional guidelines: for example, in each fare level revision he could be asked to 'load' fare increases on to the railways rather than the buses according to some predetermined criterion, so as to exploit the market that is less sensitive to price changes and protect the poorer people who tend to travel by bus. Normally, however, structure changes (like a move to a flat fare) and special concessions (like free fares for pensioners) should be reviewed and decided upon separately. This could be done by the operator putting forward specific proposals to the council (either on his own initiative or in response to a special request) for evaluation and decision in the way suggested in the last chapter.

Such changes decided upon outside the overall framework — whether in service level or fare structure, or through the introduction of a special concession — could be incorporated into the indexing procedure simply by altering the costs in the 'base' budget so as to account for the revised service level, and changing the 'base' subsidy in a similar proportion or to reflect a new decision about the triangle. The index linked multiplier procedure would then continue to operate in the same way as before.

3.9 Transport policies and programmes

These proposals would fit in particularly well with the new procedure referred to earlier (p. 18) under which local authorities in England and Wales are required to submit annually to central government their Transport Policies and Programmes (TPPs), as the basis for the allocation of a supplementary transport block grant. The TPPs are intended to include five year expenditure programmes, rolled forward each year, and drawn up in a way which reflects the council's broad strategies and objectives. Moreover, among its many aims the new procedure is intended to eliminate the bias towards capital expenditure inherent in the previous system, under which grants from central government were on the whole only made available to finance specific capital projects.

This is right in line with the above suggestions that local authorities should determine five year rolling programmes of revenue subsidy for public transport, following careful consideration of a wide range of objectives. Moreover, putting forward a clear case for the chosen subsidy level in this way would also put the council in a good position to lay stress in the TPP on the fact that the proposed expenditure should be met by central government grant rather than local rates so as to minimise adverse effects on income distribution.

Against this background it is interesting to review briefly how the main conurbations in England and Wales handled fares policy in the first round of TPPs which were submitted in July 1974 for grant in 1975—76. Not too much was expected from these first submissions, particularly as local government outside London had only just been reorganised. Further, fares policy is a wholly new field for the metropolitan county councils, so it is not surprising that most TPPs reported that policies in this area were still being worked out. Nevertheless, many interesting ideas emerged. For the immediate future, all the metropolitan county councils and the Greater London Council proposed increasing revenue support for public transport. Two of them (South Yorkshire and Merseyside) proposed that fares should be held at their current levels in 1975—76, implying a very high subsidy multiplier.[13]

The West Midlands TPP adopted an interesting approach starting from an assumption that only £6·7 million of extra grant (at constant November 1973 prices) would be likely to be available from central government over and above what would be needed to finance 'committed' expenditure. The claims of capital expenditure for highways and public transport were judged of higher priority than further revenue support for the Passenger Transport Executive, and to require the whole of the uncommitted £6·7 million. It was therefore recommended that fares should be increased so as to keep the executive's deficit at the 1974—75 level of £6 million at constant prices (one sixth of its estimated operating costs of £36 million) — implying a subsidy multiplier of one. This level of subsidy was regarded as 'committed' since the Passenger Transport Executive had advised that it would be impossible to increase fares by a larger amount.

But perhaps the most innovative approach to fares policy was the Greater Manchester Council's proposal to tie increases in bus fares to the growth in the cost of living (though this does have the disadvantages already mentioned of being a fares control rather than a subsidy control procedure). It was estimated in the TPP that this policy would lead to a real growth (at constant November 1973 prices) in support for bus fares from £5·85 million in 1975—76 to £9·82 million in 1979—80. The former figure represents about one fifth of bus operating costs, which gives an indication of how long it might be possible to maintain the policy. If, for example, cost inflation were to run at an average rate of 20 per cent a year over a long period and the fares multiplier stayed effectively at three quarters (as suggested earlier), it would take twenty five years for the subsidy to grow to three quarters of operating costs. [14] If that situation were to arise, the cost savings that would result from a switch to free bus fares might well be sufficient to justify such a move. This reinforces the point made earlier that an index linked subsidy mechanism should not be an absolute rule, but a flexible procedure based on regular monitoring and review of the relationship between the growth in subsidy and the growth in the chosen external index.

In this first year of the scheme, the government accepted the desirability of funding at least part of the required revenue subsidies from central rather than local taxation. A total of £140 million of revenue support (at November 1974 prices) required by the forty six counties in England was accepted as ranking for the transport supplementary grant. No less than £122 million of that total related to London Transport's deficit, in respect of which the grant by the government to the Greater London Council was some £53 million. However, in announcing the level of grant towards revenue support in 1975–76, the government made it clear that this was only envisaged as a temporary measure. 'In line with their overall policy of seeking to limit public expenditure, including expenditure by local authorities, the Government's aim is that bus operations in general shall move much closer towards a position of commercial viability. By 1978–79 the Government do not intend to accept more than £50 million (at November 73 prices) of such costs for grant.' [15]

Two points are worth noting about that statement. The first is the implicit preKeynesian approach to public expenditure, with its failure to recognise the distinction that needs to be drawn between transfer payments like fares subsidies, and other public expenditures whose growth may need to be restricted to ease pressure on real resources. The second point is that the £50 million quoted in the statement is equivalent to some £65 million at November 1974 prices, which means that the government's intention is to reduce the real value of its grant for revenue support by more than one half between 1975–76 and 1978–79. This will require most local authorities to increase either fares, or rates, or both, at a very much faster rate than the rate of inflation over that period. It remains to be seen whether the government will be able to hold to that intention.

3.10 Public transport as a social service industry: a new approach

Bringing together the discussion in this and the previous chapter, a number of principles have been suggested for the development of a new approach to the control of fare levels. These could be summarised as follows:

1   The day-to-day management of public transport services should be delegated by the local council to a public transport operator, under a substantial degree of accountability and independent responsibility, defined in more detail than they normally are in the laws and statutes that lay down the relative responsibilities of governing bodies and operators.

2   The operator's day-to-day management actions should be governed by the maximisation of the achievement of a single output oriented goal, chosen so as to fit in with the local council's wider social and economic objectives: subject to whatever additional guidelines the local authority might wish to lay down.

3   It is not a sin for the operator to make a loss. Indeed, the local council should be able (if it wishes) to require him to make a loss as a positive act of policy. More generally, the management procedures should enable the local authority to make positive triangular choices as to the balance between fare, subsidy and service levels, anywhere in the range between the social service and nationalised industry approaches (including at either end of the spectrum).

4   The operator should be given a clear set of groundrules to enable him to plan in advance on the basis of a firm awareness of the amount of income he will receive, both from fares revenue and subsidy.

5   The procedures should give both the local authority and the operator incentives to improved performance – with regard to the effective achievement of objectives as well as the efficient implementation of agreed programmes.

An approach based on these principles might be called the social service industry approach, as a compromise between the nationalised industry and welfare state approaches described earlier.

APPENDIX

3A.1 The effects of index linked subsidy and fares control procedures

By definition, costs (C), fares income (F), and subsidy (S) at time t are always related by the equation

$$C = F + S$$

provided that profits are not actually made — a possibility which is excluded from the analysis.

The following calculations assume that C is growing at a constant continuous compound growth rate r, so that

$$C = C_0 e^{rt} \text{ at time } t$$

3A.2 Control over subsidy

If subsidy grows at a constant multiple n of the growth in costs, then

$$S = S_0 e^{nrt} \text{ at time } t$$

The point at which fares start to fall can be calculated by finding the maximum of

$$F = C_0 e^{rt} - S_0 e^{nrt}$$

Thus

$$\frac{dF}{dt} = rC_0 e^{rt} - nrS_0 e^{nrt}$$

$$= 0$$

when

$$\Theta_0 e^{rt} = n \, e^{nrt} \quad (\Theta_0 = C_0/S_0)$$

or

$$t = \frac{\log \Theta_0 - \log n}{r(n-1)} \tag{3A.1}$$

Fares are free when

$$C_0 e^{rt} = S_0 e^{nrt}$$

or

$$t = \frac{\log \Theta_0}{r(n-1)} \tag{3A.2}$$

Illustrative figures derived from equations (3A.1) and (3A.2) are shown in Table 3A.1, assuming that subsidies initially account for 10 per cent of total costs (i.e. $\Theta_0 = 10$) and that costs inflate at an annual rate of 20 per cent. (It should be noted that this latter assumption means that the continuous compound growth rate r is log 1·2, not 0·2.)

Table 3A.1

Effect of subsidy control

	Subsidy multiplier (n)			
	3	2	1½	1¼
Time (years) until:				
fares start to fall	3	9	21	46
free fares	6	13	25	50

If $n = 1$, the subsidy will stay at a constant proportion of total costs (one tenth in this instance). With $n < 1$, the subsidy proportion will gradually decline, though a self-financing position is never reached. It can be calculated, for example, that if r stays constant at log 1·2, the subsidy will have dropped from 10 per cent to 5 per cent of total costs after five, eight and fifteen years respectively, according to whether n is set at a quarter, one half or three quarters.

3A.3   Control over fares

If fares income grows at a constant multiple m of the growth in costs, then

$$F = F_0 e^{mrt} \text{ at time } t$$

If we define

$$\phi = 1 - \frac{1}{\Theta}$$

as the proportion of fares income to total costs, then

$$\phi = \frac{F_0 e^{mrt}}{C_0 e^{rt}}$$

therefore

$$\phi e^{rt} = \phi_0 e^{mrt}$$

58

therefore

$$t = \frac{\log \phi_0 - \log \phi}{r (1-m)} \qquad (3A.3)$$

This equation can be used to calculate how long it would take for subsidies to reach certain proportions of total costs. Table 3A.2 shows the results for quarter, half and three quarters of total costs, for different values of the fares multiplier (m) less than one, and again assuming that $\Theta_0 = 10$ and $r = \log 1 \cdot 2$. If $m = 1$, the subsidy again remains at a constant proportion (one tenth) of total costs. With $m > 1$, fares income will soon be high enough to cover costs in full — after two years when $m = 1\frac{1}{4}$, and only one year when $m = 1\frac{1}{2}$.

Table 3A.2

Effect of fares control

	fares multiplier (m)		
	$\frac{1}{4}$	$\frac{1}{2}$	$\frac{3}{4}$
time (years) for subsidies to reach:			
$\frac{1}{4}$ of total costs	1	2	4
$\frac{1}{2}$ of total costs	4	6	13
$\frac{3}{4}$ of total costs	9	14	28

Notes

[1] *The Reshaping of British Railways,* HMSO, 1963.

[2] A. Grey, *The Role of Local Government in Fares Policy,* op.cit.

[3] *Nationalised Industries: A Review of Financial and Economic Objectives,* Cmnd 3437, 1967.

[4] The latter evidence is reviewed in M.A. Kemp, 'Some Evidence of Transit Demand Elasticities', *Transportation,* April 1973.

[5] See R. Dobson et al., op.cit.

[6] See, for example, P.B. Goodwin, 'Generalised Time and the Problem of Equity in Transport Studies', *Transportation,* April 1974.

[7] T.A. Domencich and G. Kraft, *Free Transit,* Heath Lexington Books, 1970.

[8] P.B. Goodwin, 'Some Data on the Effects of Free Public Transport', *Transportation Planning and Technology,* vol. 1(3), 1973.

[9] Papers 5 and 6 in *Symposium on Public Transport Fare Structure,* Transport and Road Research Laboratory Supplementary Reports 36UC and 37UC, 1974.

[10] In 1975 public transport costs in Great Britain were inflating at a much faster rate than this, though inflation rates in most other European countries and in North America were much lower.

[11] This can be calculated from the figures given in the *Monthly Digest of Statistics,* HMSO.

[12] See, for example, *Changing Directions,* Report of the Independent Commission on Transport, 1974.

[13] It can be calculated that the multiplier would be approximately equal to costs divided by subsidy in the base year 1974—75, i.e. ϕ_0 using the terminology in the appendix to this chapter.

[14] This can be shown by substituting the relevant figures in equation (3A.3) of the appendix.

[15] Department of Environment Circular 171/74, para. 25.

4 The Impact of Changes in Fare Levels

In the light of the suggestions in the last chapter, we now consider how the operator can decide the amount by which he should change the general level of fares in order to fill the gap between costs and subsidy. The local council and the operator will, of course, also be concerned with the wider impact of fares changes on the prospects for achieving the full range of their objectives. However, these wider implications — such as the impact on traffic congestion discussed earlier, and the social effects which will be explored in detail in Chapter 6 — should already have been taken into account in deciding the broad structure of fares and special concessions, and in determining how the fares—subsidy—service level triangle is to be drawn. Here we are concerned with the impact on demand, and thereby receipts, of the general changes in the fare level that will be required once the overall fares policy has been decided.

4.1 Influences on demand

Public transport demand is influenced not only by changes in fare levels, but also by a variety of other factors. Some of these will be policy instruments under the local council's control, e.g. changes in service level, and traffic restraint measures. Others will relate to underlying trends in population, employment, social structure and behaviour, land use, and so on. Then there will be movements in the relative prices of other goods and services — the prices of competitive services, like the motor car, will be particularly important here. And there will also be the windfalls and disasters mentioned in the last chapter such as sharp changes in petrol prices and strikes.

Many empirical models have been constructed in an attempt to wrestle with at least some of these factors. So far perhaps the most comprehensive has been the model designed by Charles Rivers Associates for their Boston Study.[1] They estimated eight equations (for four journey purposes, separately for public transport and car in each case) relating numbers of trips to several independent variables. Logarithmic, linear and mixed log linear cross sectional demand functions were estimated by a constrained multiple regression procedure, intended to avoid the problems of multi-collinearity with the mixed log linear equations. The independent variables included time and travel costs for both modes, distinguishing getting to the vehicle from travelling on it in each case. Other variables relating to employment, car ownership, and household income were also used.

Another comprehensive approach to cross sectional modelling of transport demand, also developed in the United States, is known as 'abstract mode' modelling.[2] Demand is expressed directly in terms of the attributes of transport modes (such as their speed, frequency of service and cost) regardless of whether they might be described institutionally as bus, train, car, etc. The equations are usually logarithmic, and express the number of trips by any one mode between one place and another, in terms of the fastest journey time and cheapest cost by any mode, and the relative times and costs by the mode in question. Other variables like population, employment, and income are also included.

Apart from conventional transport models (which I have argued in Chapter 1 are inappropriate for considering the impact of fares changes) the approaches tried to date in Britain have been much less comprehensive. The Department of the Environment has published time series estimates relating, through a logarithmic equation, the number of bus trips in ten British towns to the real fare level (money fares corrected for the change in the price level), the number of vehicle miles run (a quality of service indicator) and a residual time trend.[3] London Transport has also adopted an approach relating the change in receipts to similar independent variables.[4] The main differences were the treatment of fares changes as dummy variables, and the inclusion of parameters to allow for the effect of changes in the weather and in real incomes. Equations were also estimated separately for bus and train, and for weekdays and weekends.

Neither the complex cross sectional nor the simpler time series models are yet able to provide workable management tools to assist the operator in taking decisions on general fare levels. The former can provide reliable evidence about important policy issues such as the likely response of different income groups to fares changes. But they are a poor aid to forward planning if the estimated relationships are not stable through time. This problem could in theory be tackled by pooling time series and cross sectional models, so that changes through time in the estimated cross sectional relationships are revealed directly by the analysis. But the turbulence of the underlying influences on transport demand is likely to make the time series unstable as well. And the level of technical ingenuity required to get round these problems would make the models even more complicated and thereby of even less relevance to urban governments faced with the task of taking actual and regular decisions on fares changes.

The most practicable solution would seem to be an approach on the following lines:

1   Cross sectional demand models should be used primarily by the local authority as an aid to determining the social and environmental implications of alternative fares policies, in order to provide a basis for deciding whether the policy on general fares levels should be changed, and whether new fares structures or special concessions should be introduced. Both the choice and application of these models should be governed by judgements as to whether the estimated relationships are likely to be stable through time.

2   The operator should be concerned mainly with the effects of changes in the fare level on overall demand and receipts, using the evidence from both time series and cross sectional models where available, supplemented by his own commercial experience about how passengers have responded to previous fares changes. Other underlying influences on aggregate demand should be allowed for by reaching agreement with the council as to what, if any, adjustments need to be made to the separately identified impact of the fares change.

Some new cross sectional demand models, to meet the first of these points, are developed later (Chapter 6). This chapter is concerned with the second point, and discusses certain rules and formulae that the operator might use in working out the direct impact of fares changes on aggregate demand and receipts, other things being equal.

4.2   Demand elasticities

Whatever method is chosen to measure the response of demand to price changes, it will have to be able to indicate that the impact of (say) a 5p reduction in a fare value will be much greater if the fare was 10p than if it was £1 before the change. The method will also be much simpler if it is independent of the measuring units being employed; whether prices are measured in pounds, marks, or dollars, or demand in passenger miles or journeys, for example. Such considerations imply that proportionate rather than absolute changes have to be considered; and have led to the adoption of the concept of *elasticity* as a term of art denoting the relationship between the proportionate change in quantity and the proportionate change in price that has caused it.

Elasticity is, in fact, a general concept which holds an important place in economic theory, and is used to measure the interrelationship between changes in any two interdependent variables, not just price and quantity. But unfortunately, at least as far as fares policy is concerned, a fair amount on confusion seems to surround the concept both in the theory and in the practical application. This means that in order to determine the best way of using the concept in fares policy, a critical appraisal is needed of the various ways in which it has been formulated and applied.

This appraisal, which is carried out in Appendix 4A.1, leads to the conclusion that the choice lies between the *line* and *arc* elasticities, represented by the symbol η, and defined respectively by the formulae

$$q = \eta p \qquad (4.1)$$

$$1 + q = (1 + p)^{\eta} \qquad (4.2)$$

where *p, q,* denote proportional changes in the absolute price level *(P)* and quantity demanded *(Q)*.

The best method will depend on which of these formulae gives the best representation of the true relationship between price and quantity over the range of changes being planned for and implemented. There is no *a priori* reason for preferring one approach to the other, and each operator must make his own choice in the light of the maximum amount of information about the nature of that relationship. This chapter uses the arc elasticity approach purely to illustrate certain methods and procedures, without taking sides in any way. If an operator decides that the line elasticity is more appropriate to the situation he is faced with, the same methods can be applied to obtain corresponding results.

Since demand normally goes up when price goes down, and vice versa, the arc elasticity will usually be negative. If it were zero, demand would be unaffected by the price change, whatever its size. As the absolute value of the elasticity (namely $-\eta$) gets bigger, the effect on demand of price changes becomes more substantial. When it is greater than one, this response is big enough to mean that a reduction in price will actually lead to an increase in revenue (though this well known result does not apply in this way to the line elasticity approach, as Appendix 4A.1 shows).

For small price changes the various methods of measuring elasticity give approximately equal results; and studies in a number of industrialised countries have shown that they tend to range from between -0.1 to -0.7 for the response of public transport demand to fares changes. They tend to be at the higher end of the range when alternative choices are open to the traveller, such as in off peak periods (when unlike the work journey, he can easily choose not to make the trip at all) or for short distance bus journeys (when he has the option of walking instead).

The elasticity values will also depend on what assumptions have been made about other influences on demand. The influence of the movement in the relative prices of other goods and services is sometimes allowed for by using the concept of *cross elasticity,* defined as the relationship between the proportionate change in demand for the quantity being considered and the proportionate change in one of these other prices. It has already been suggested that any allowance that may need to be made for external influences on demand (including those resulting from the cross elasticity phenomenon) should be considered separately. In addition, however, there may be cross elasticity effects internal to the fare level change being introduced. For example, passengers in graduated or zonal fares systems may shorten their journeys so as to avoid the full fares increase, and some rail passengers may divert to bus if they have suffered a larger fares increase. It would in most cases be appropriate to assume that the elasticities are calculated in a way which makes implicit allowance for all cross elasticities inherent in the fares changes themselves, so that it is the net impact on demand of the package of fares changes that is being measured. However, if major differential price changes are being considered for different parts of the market between which significant transfers of passengers are likely to occur, then it may well be necessary to introduce explicit assumptions about cross elasticity. For example, if an operator increases bus and rail fares by 10 per cent and 20 per cent respectively, and if this causes a 5 per cent gross loss of bus passengers offset by a 2 per cent increase caused by people transferring from rail so as to avoid paying the relatively higher fare, then the net impact on demand for bus travel of the fares changes is a drop of 3 per cent. But because the transfer of passengers from rail to bus has in this case been quite large, it might be better to work with the gross arc elasticity (−0·54), together with a separate measure of cross elasticity,[5] rather than with the net arc elasticity of −0·32.

4.3   Inflation

In order to investigate the practical implications of using the arc elasticity approach, it is first necessary to consider how to take account of inflation. The most straightforward approach to estimating the effects of fares changes in an inflationary climate is to assume that demand is only affected by changes in relative prices. Thus, for example, if the general price level rises by 20 per cent as a result of inflation, and if fares are increased by 20 per cent, there is no effect on demand as there has been no change in the real fare level (that is, in the level of fares relative to the price of other goods and services). Similarly, if fares are held, there will.be an increase in demand caused by a reduction in the real fare level; and fares would have to be increased by more than 20 per cent to cause a fall off in demand.

The change in the money price of fares can be converted into a change in the real price by multiplying by an index representing the change in the general price level. In Britain, the most appropriate index is the general index of retail prices. This is published monthly by central government, broken down into a number of components.[6] Although it is a national index, it will give a good indication of the changes in the general price level in any one town unless there are significant variations in the consumption pattern from one part of the country to another. If any one local council were to feel that its own area was atypical, it would have to decide whether the differences were substantial enough to warrant introducing some kind of modification to the national index. In theory, a correction could also be made to allow for the fact that fares form part of the retail price index. But since they account for only a small proportion of the index (2·5 per cent in 1973), the correction would not be worth making, particularly as the error resulting from not making that correction would almost certainly be smaller than the error involved in forecasting the value of the index itself.

The amount by which fares are to be increased should allow for the fact that this increase comes with a jerk at one point in time, whereas to all intents and purposes the retail price index increases continually. Hence the real fare level will decline continuously after the initial jump, until the next fares increase. Appendix 4A.2 shows that if p is the planned proportional increase in the money fare level at the beginning of the budget year, then the proportional increase in receipts (f) in the budget year compared with the preceding year will be approximately given by

$$1 + f = (1 + r)^{-\eta} (1 + p)^{\eta + 1} \qquad (4.3)$$

where r is an estimate of the current annual rate of inflation in the retail price index.

Equation (4.3) was actually derived on a more general basis and would apply to receipts and fares changes between any two periods of time of equal intervals, whether they be yearly, six monthly or whatever. But in practice, unless rates of inflation were very high, it would be convenient to plan for just one annual fares increase at the beginning of each financial year.

The procedure might work as follows. The operator would agree with the council, at the time when the budget for the following financial year was being prepared in, say, October, what figure should be assumed for the current rate of growth in the retail price index. This could, perhaps, be taken as what is thought to be the best general measure of the current rate of inflation: namely the change during the previous six months of all items in the index apart from seasonally sensitive food prices, expressed on an annual basis. The necessary fares increase to fill the gap between costs and subsidy could then be calculated and planned for implementation at the start of the financial year, the following April.

To illustrate, if the current rate of inflation r is 20 per cent; if η is taken as -0.3; and if receipts are also required to grow by 20 per cent to fill the gap between costs and subsidy; then it can be calculated from Equation (4.3) that fares will have to be increased by 20 per cent at the beginning of the year – thus confirming that the equation is consistent with the hypothesis that on average there is no drop in demand in the budget year if the price increase matches the inflation rate. However, if receipts are required to grow at a faster rate than inflation, the required price increase will have to be higher still, and vice versa. A 30 per cent receipts increase, for example, requires a 35 per cent fares increase, using the same assumptions for η and r.

If no allowance had been made for inflation, the equation corresponding to (4.3) would have been

$$1 + f = (1 + p)^{\eta + 1}$$

This shows that much higher fares increases (of 30 per cent and 45 per cent respectively) would have been required to yield the receipts increases of 20 per cent and 30 per cent. More generally the factor $(1 + r)^{-\eta}$, which is greater than one, represents the additional bonus to receipts that results from a given rate of inflation. With $\eta = -0.3$ and $r = 0.2$, the value of this factor is 1.06. This means that receipts for the whole year would be 6 per cent higher than the previous year if fares were held (i.e. $p = 0$). The factor $(1 + r)^{-\eta}$ also represents the additional bonus to demand resulting from a given inflation rate, implying that demand will have grown by 6 per cent on average during the year if fares are held at the beginning.

It should be stressed that this represents the average change in demand for the whole of the budget year compared with the whole of the current year. Excluding seasonal effects (like the weather) and other external influences, the actual demand during the year will drop initially as a result of the fares increase at the beginning, but then gradually rise as a result of the continual erosion of the fare level in comparison with the growth in the general price level. It can be shown that the proportionate change in demand q at time t during the year, compared with the position at the beginning of the year, is given by

$$1 + q = (1 + r)^{-\eta t} (1 + p)^{\eta} \tag{4.4}$$

where r this time is the estimated rate of inflation during the budget year rather than the current rate of inflation.[7]

4.4   Detailed impact on demand

Unfortunately, however, Equations (4.3) and (4.4) can only be applied directly to work out the total impact on demand and receipts of fares changes, if they are applied in equal proportions to all fare values, and if the demand elasticities are similar at these different values. In practice neither of these assumptions is likely to hold (except in the case of changes in fare level to a flat fare structure, when the first assumption will hold by definition since there is only one fare value). For example, the changes in the March 1975 revision to London's bus and underground fares ranged from a reduction in some bus fares to a doubling of some underground fares, which is by no means an unusual mixture for a change in fare levels in a graduated fare structure. Moreover, as was indicated earlier, variations in elasticities between short and long distance passengers (who pay different fare values unless there is a flat fare structure) can be quite marked. And elasticities will also vary between styles of service. London's underground passengers, for example, are far less sensitive to price increases than bus passengers, probably because they are willing to pay more for the faster and more reliable service, and on average are better off anyway. Based on their own experience, London Transport were assuming in 1974 overall elasticities of −0·1 for the underground, but three times as much (−0·3) for the buses. LT's experience is also that elasticities are much higher outside peak hours: for buses they were assumed to be −0·4 in the off peak, and −0·2 in the peak.

Yet another problem could arise in this area if passengers responded differently to fares increases and fares reductions, implying different elasticities at the same point according to the direction of the price change. This would be a particularly awkward dilemma in the approach suggested here, because of the need to take account at the same time of increases in real fare levels at the beginning of the year, and reductions during the year resulting from the continual increase in the general price level. However, since there is no empirical evidence to support that proposition, we will continue to assume the hypothesis of a smooth constant elasticity demand curve, which lies behind the arc elasticity concept.

In general, the total proportional change in demand must be calculated as a weighted average of the changes in each of the separate market segments which have incurred different fares increases p_i or for which different elasticities η_i have been assumed. If a_i are the proportions of total journeys sold in each of these segments (with $\Sigma a_i = 1$), then this weighted average is given by

$$q = \Sigma a_i q_i$$

therefore

$$1+q = \Sigma a_i \, (1+q_i) \qquad (4.5)$$
$$= \Sigma a_i \, (1+r)^{-\eta_i t} \, (1+p_i)^{\eta_i} \qquad \text{[from (4.4)]}$$

It is interesting to use this equation to estimate the impact on demand of the changes effected to London's bus fares in March 1975. As already noted, these changes ranged from decreases to substantial increases at different fare values. The relevant figures are given in the table below.

Table 4.1

London Transport bus fare changes (March 1975)

Fares (pence)		% change (p_i)	% of total fare paying passenger journeys (a_i)
old (P_i)	new		
3	4	+33	41·34
5	7	+40	30·94
8	10	+25	12·98
10	13	+30	6·89
10	15	+50	4·00
13	15	+15	1·39
15	15	0	0·33
18	15	−17	0·05
20	15	−25	0·01
off 12 peak max.	12	0	2·07

Source: London Transport.

If the elasticity η was assumed to be constant at $-0\cdot3$ for all fare values, and the inflation in the retail price index taken to grow at a constant annual rate of 20 per cent between March 1975 and March 1976, then

$$1+q = 1\cdot2^{0\cdot3t}\Sigma a_i\,(1+p_i)^{-0\cdot3}$$

$$= 0\cdot92 \times 1\cdot2^{0\cdot3t}$$

Hence on those assumptions passenger journeys would have dropped by 8 per cent at the beginning of the year ($t = 0$), but climbed back to be 5 per cent down in the middle ($t = \frac{1}{2}$) and only 3 per cent down by the end ($t = 1$).

A number of other interesting points can be deduced from these equations. For example, we can discover what the values of η and r would have to be in order to claim back by the end of the year all the passengers lost as a result of the fares increase at the beginning. Thus for the London Transport bus fares increase, we need to find the solution to equation (4.5) when $q = 0$ and $t = 1$, namely

$$0\cdot92\,(1+r)^{-\eta} = 1$$

Hence if $\eta = -0\cdot3$, a rate of inflation *(r)* of 32 per cent would be sufficient to reduce the 8 per cent loss in passengers at the beginning of the year to nothing by the end.

4.5 Detailed impact on receipts

The total impact on receipts must also be calculated as a weighted average of the changes in each of the market segments to which different fares changes have been applied or for which different elasticities have been assumed. But this time the calculations are complicated by the fact that the proportional changes must be applied to a_iP_i in each market segment (P_i being the fare value) rather than just to a_i. Hence the weighted average proportional change in receipts is given by:

$$f = \Sigma f_i\,a_iP_i/\Sigma a_iP_i$$

therefore

$$1+f = \Sigma(1+f_i)a_iP_i/\Sigma a_iP_i$$

therefore

$$(\Sigma a_iP_i)\,(1+f) = \Sigma(1+r)^{-\eta_i}\,(1+p_i)^{\eta_i\,+1}\,a_iP_i \qquad (4.6)$$

Equation (4.6) is, of course, much more complicated than (4.3), the degree of added complexity depending on how many different market segments have to be assumed. However, once the figures have been settled, the formula is conceptually simple and most operators should be able to arrange for the necessary calculations to be done mechanically.

If we apply Equation (4.6) to the March 1975 change in London Transport's bus fares, making the same assumptions as before ($\eta_i = -0.3$ for all i, $r = 0.2$), then by using the figures in Table 4.1, it can be calculated that

$$1+f = 1.28$$

In other words, on these assumptions bus fares income would be expected to increase by about 28 per cent as a result of the fares change. This means extra bus receipts of some £18·5 million in a complete year (they amounted to £66 million in total in 1974): a much higher figure than London Transport's own estimate of a yield of £13·9 million in extra bus receipts.[8] However, in many ways it is surprising that the two forecasts are not more widely apart, in view of the different assumptions that London Transport is bound to have made about inflation, elasticities, and underlying trends in demand apart from those influenced by the fares change.

As far as the latter point is concerned, it was suggested earlier that the operator and local authority should reach agreement between them at the beginning of the year as to how these underlying trends are to be allowed for. In periods of economic recession (such as the energy crisis and harsh economic climate experienced at the time of this particular fares change) it would seem sensible to assume that these trends cancel each other out, since the factors such as London's falling population that cause a decline in demand are likely to be offset by other influences. Moreover, rising car ownership, which has traditionally been associated with the declining demand for bus travel, is no longer likely to be such an important influence.

If a zero underlying trend had been agreed in this way, there are only two variables that influence the forecast increase in receipts, namely the elasticity and the inflation rate. The figure of 20 per cent for r used in the above calculation was a good enough approximation to the current annual rate of inflation when the fares increase was decided in November 1974. Hence if the forecast of £18·5 million turned out to be wrong, it would have been logical to assume that this was because the elasticity had been incorrectly estimated.[9] Under this approach the operator would therefore have revised the elasticity to match the change in receipts actually observed, and used the new figure in the following year's forecasts.

In practice, the operator will wish to derive the required proportional increases in fares p_i from the target proportional increase in revenue f that is needed to fill the gap between costs and subsidy: and not the other way round as is necessary with Equation (4.6). The best way to allow for this would be first of all to apply Equation (4.3) (which can be used either way round) separately to the main market segments in which different elasticities are assumed to hold (such as buses and underground in London), thus showing the average increase in prices that would be necessary to yield the target increases in revenue that are needed in each market.

It would be wise here (unless this were to conflict with some other objective) to require a higher target increase in revenue for the markets in which lower (absolute) elasticities apply, since this would require a smaller fare increase to yield the same amount of revenue, or by the same token lose less passenger miles for each extra £1 of revenue gained from the fares increase. This has, for example, been the practice over the last few years in London, where fares revisions have involved higher increases for the underground than for the buses.

The final step would be to use the average fare increases derived from the revenue targets as constraints affecting the amount by which any one fare value should be increased, within each of the markets for which different elasticities have been assumed to hold. The aim should be to keep each of the individual fare increases as close as possible to the average of the relevant market segment. But where this cannot be done too easily on practical grounds, a certain amount of juggling with Equation (4.6), on a trial and error basis, may be needed.

APPENDICES

4A.1 Measuring elasticity: which approach is best?

This appendix considers the most appropriate way of measuring the elasticity of demand with respect to price in fares policy, by reviewing four different methods that have been used, and considering a possible new approach as well. It should be noted that the analysis is sufficiently general to be applicable to other types of elasticity and in other policy areas.

4A.1.1 *Point elasticity*

The point elasticity defines the relationship between price *(P)* and quantity *(Q)* at any point in terms of the parameter

$$\eta = \frac{dQ}{dP} \cdot \frac{P}{Q} \qquad\qquad (4A.1)$$

Essentially this measures the ratio between an infinitesimally small proportional change in quantity dQ/Q and the infinitesimally small proportional change in price dP/P that has caused it.

The revenue F at any point is given by

$$F = PQ$$

therefore

$$\frac{dF}{dP} = P\frac{dQ}{dP} + Q$$

therefore

$$dF = (\eta + 1)Q\, dP$$

This equation proves the well known property that a marginal increase in price at any point will lead to an increase, no change, or decrease in revenue, according to whether the absolute value of the point elasticity (namely $-\eta$) is less than, equal to, or greater than one.

It is vital to be aware that Equation (4A.1) only says something about what happens at a point. It cannot by itself be used to measure the relationship between finite changes in prices and quantity. (If $\eta = -1$, for example, the assumption that a 30 per cent price rise leads to a 30 per cent fall off in demand, implies a 9 per cent drop in revenue rather than no change). Such relationships can only be estimated from prior assumptions about the likely level of demand at different price levels, over the full range of the variables being considered: assumptions which are usually represented in economic theory by drawing a so called demand curve to describe how price and quantity relate to each other over the relevant range. However, since there is as yet little reliable empirical evidence about what the demand curve looks like, the simplest and most practicable approach may be to supplement the point elasticity definition with further assumptions about the shape and position of the demand curve over the range of variables in which we are interested.

A general hypothesis which seems most likely to be consistent with empirical evidence is that price and quantity are related in such a way that the demand curve is of the shape shown on p. 74.

That general hypothesis will be used below as one of the tests of the suitability of the three other common methods of defining and measuring elasticity. Described in more detail, it asserts not only that price changes

Fig. 4A.1   Hypothetical demand curve for fares changes

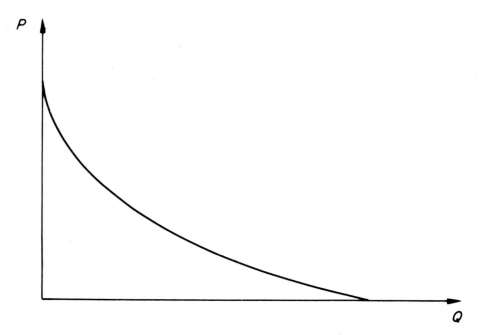

will be in the opposite direction to the resulting changes in demand (so that η is always negative), but also that they will have a greater impact on demand when prices are low than when they are high. (This latter point makes the demand curve convex towards the origin, as illustrated.) Finally, the curve meets the axes at finite values of P and Q (i.e. there will be a price high enough to choke off all demand, and a finite demand when fares are free).

It can be shown that just two of these conditions — that η is negative, and that the demand curve cuts the P axis at a finite value of P — imply that $(-\eta)$ is increasing as P increases. Its value will also tend to infinity as Q tends to zero; so there will come a point on the demand curve at which $\eta = -1$, beyond which further price increases will cause a decline in revenue. The more convex the demand curve, the slower will be the rate of increase in $-\eta$; and that point of maximum revenue will thus be reached later.

4A.1.2   Line elasticity

The most common way of measuring the impact of future price changes on demand is by means of the ratio

$$\eta_1 = \frac{\text{proportional change in quantity}}{\text{proportional change in price}}$$

This measure owes its popularity to its simplicity and to the fact that it can be used as a rough approximation for the point elasticity η for very small changes. However, the assumption that the ratio is constant over a finite range implies

$$\frac{Q-Q_0}{Q_0} = \eta_1 \frac{P-P_0}{P_0}$$

for all changes from the initial position (P_0, Q_0) to any new position (P,Q) in that range, or

$$Q = Q_0/P_0 \; \eta_1 P + (1 - \eta_1)Q_0 \qquad (4A.2)$$

This means that the demand curve (4A.2) is assumed to be a straight line over the range of the price changes being considered; which is why I have used the title *line elasticity* to describe this approach. Thus an inevitable consequence of the line elasticity approach is that it is inconsistent with the general hypothesis about the convex shape of the demand curve.

The main problem with a linear demand curve is the very fast fall off in demand reflected in the sharp growth in the point elasticity, so that the points of maximum revenue (where $\eta = -1$) – and beyond that of zero gain in revenue – are reached much sooner than one would intuitively expect.

Those points can be derived by working with the quantities p, q, defined as proportional changes in the initial levels of price (P_0) and quantity (Q_0).

Thus the new receipts are given by

$$R = (1 + p)(1 + q)R_0$$

$$= \left\{1 + (1 + \eta_1)p + \eta_1 p^2\right\} R_0 \text{ (since } q = \eta_1 p)$$

therefore

$$\frac{dR}{dp} = (1 + \eta_1 + 2 \eta_1 p)R_0$$

Since receipts reach a maximum when $\frac{dR}{dp} = 0$, and the total gain in revenue is zero when $R = R_0$, those points are given respectively by the equations

$$p = -\frac{1 + \eta_1}{2 \eta_1} \qquad (4A.3)$$

and

$$p = - \frac{1 + \eta_1}{\eta_1} \qquad (4A.4)$$

Thus, for example, if η_1 is set at -0.5, revenue will have reached its maximum value when prices have risen by only 50 per cent ($p = 0.5$), and there will be a loss in total revenue compared with the starting position if prices are more than doubled ($p = 1.0$) — neither of which seems very likely.

4A.1.3 *Mid-point elasticity*

This concept was introduced to counteract the high fall off in demand for large fare increases experienced with the line elasticity. It involves expressing the changes in price and quantity as percentages of the midpoint between the new and old positions, and defining the midpoint elasticity η_m as the (constant) ratio between them. Thus

$$\frac{Q-Q_0}{\frac{1}{2}(Q+Q_0)} = \eta_m \frac{P-P_0}{\frac{1}{2}(P+P_0)}$$

This equation can be expressed as

$$(Q-aQ_0)(P+aP_0) = -4\eta_m/(1-\eta_m)^2 P_0 Q_0 \qquad (4A.5)$$

where $a = (1+\eta_m)/(1-\eta_m)$. Being a rectangular hyperbola (with asymptotes $Q = aQ_0$ and $P = -aP_0$) this demand curve is of the right convex shape. However, it is cumbersome and rather difficult to handle. Moreover, the vertical asymptote $Q = aQ_0$ is to the right of the P axis, so the curve never gets anywhere near that axis unless either Q_0 or η_m are very small. This suggests that the absolute value of the point elasticity ($-\eta$) declines, rather than grows, as P increases, so that the point of declining revenue is never reached. This is indeed so, for the relationship between the point and midpoint elasticities can be calculated as

$$\eta = \frac{(1+p)\eta_m}{1+p+\frac{1}{4}p^2(1-\eta^2_m)}$$

And this equation confirms that ($-\eta$) declines with rising p if $0 < \eta_m < 1$, and that $\eta_m = -1$ if and only if $\eta = -1$.

However, the midpoint elasticity demand curve performs much better when considering falling rather than rising prices, since the horizontal asymptote is below the Q axis. The point at which the curve cuts the Q

axis can be calculated as $(1-\eta_m)/(1+\eta_m)Q_0$, compared with $(1-\eta_1)Q_0$ for the line elasticity. With an elasticity of $-0\cdot5$, for example, this means that free fares would yield increases in demand of 200 per cent and 50 per cent respectively.

4A.1.4 Arc elasticity

This approach starts from the hypothesis that the point elasticity is constant over the range of the curve in which we are interested. This implies the demand curve

$$\log Q = \eta \log P + k \qquad (4A.6)_\bullet$$

which is obtained by integrating Equation (4A.1). This curve is also of the right shape (convex towards the origin) and its main inconsistency with the general hypothesis is that it does not meet either of the axes (it approaches them both asymptotically). It thus performs better than the midpoint elasticity for rising prices, but worse for falling prices.

The relationship between the point elasticity and changes in price and quantity is

$$\eta = \frac{\log Q - \log Q_0}{\log P - \log P_0}$$

This ratio is called the arc elasticity — perhaps a somewhat misleading term, since η is still the point elasticity, and the relationship is only obtained as a result of assuming that η is constant.

The above equation can also be expressed as

$$\eta = \frac{\log (1+q)}{\log (1+p)}$$

or

$$1+q = (1+p)^\eta \qquad (4A.7)$$

This is a much simpler formula to use in practical calculations than the complicated expression required for the midpoint elasticity. The other important advantage of this approach in terms of simplicity is that no separate calculations have to be made for the point elasticity.

4A.1.5 Modified arc elasticity

The major problem with the arc elasticity is that it only approaches the axes asymptotically. Hence it becomes increasingly unreliable as the price changes being considered (in either direction) get bigger.

In theory it is easy to get over that problem just by shifting the vertical asymptote over to the left a distance βQ_0 (say) and lowering the horizontal asymptote a distance aP_0. It can be calculated that this would lead to the demand curve

$$1 + \frac{q}{1 + \beta} = \left(1 + \frac{p}{1 + a}\right)^{\eta}$$

With this equation the point elasticity is no longer represented by η and is not constant along the curve. As with the line elasticity, its absolute value increases as the price increases, though at a much slower rate. It can be shown that its value at the starting position (P_0, Q_0) is given by

$$\eta_0 = \frac{1 + \beta}{1 + a}\eta$$

It is clearly best to choose a and β so that they are equal, for then η will be the same as the point elasticity at the starting position. The values of a and β can then be determined to make the curves cut the axes at what seem to be reasonable points.

The most appropriate value of $a = \beta$ will also depend on the initial point elasticity $\eta = \eta_0$. The simplest solution to that conundrum is to choose

$$1 - \eta q = (1 - \eta p)^{\eta} \qquad (4A.8)$$

This involves taking $a = \beta = -(1+\eta)/\eta$, and that solution also gives reasonable answers for the points at which the curves cut the axes. This is shown by Table 4A.1, which compares the results with those that would have been found with the line elasticity approach.

Table 4A.1

Effects of modified arc and line elasticity approaches

Elasticity concept	Point at which there is	Initial point elasticity (η)			
		-0.1	-0.3	-0.5	-0.7
Modified arc	zero demand	$19.68P_0$	$8.61P_0$	$7.00P_0$	$7.55P_0$
	zero gain in revenue	$17.96P_0$	$6.52P_0$	$4.24P_0$	$3.26P_0$
	maximum revenue	$8.46P_0$	$3.38P_0$	$2.37P_0$	$1.94P_0$
	free fares	$1.11Q_0$	$1.38Q_0$	$1.83Q_0$	$2.89Q_0$
Line	zero demand	$11.00P_0$	$4.33P_0$	$3.00P_0$	$2.43P_0$
	zero gain in revenue	$10.00P_0$	$3.33P_0$	$2.00P_0$	$1.43P_0$
	maximum revenue	$5.50P_0$	$2.17P_0$	$1.50P_0$	$1.21P_0$
	free fares	$1.10Q_0$	$1.30Q_0$	$1.50Q_0$	$1.70Q_0$

Source: Equations (4A.2)–(4A.4) and (4A.8)–(4A.10).

Table 4A.1 also compares the points where receipts are at a maximum, and at which there is no gain in receipts. The formulae corresponding to those derived earlier for the line elasticity can be calculated as

$$(1 - \eta p)^{\eta - 1} \left\{ \eta - \frac{1}{\eta} + (1 + \eta)p \right\} + 1 + \frac{1}{\eta} = 0 \qquad (4A.9)$$

for maximum receipts, and

$$(1+p) \left\{ 1 - (1 - \eta p)^{\eta} \right\} + \eta p = 0 \qquad (4A.10)$$

for zero gain in revenue.

4A.1.6 *Conclusions*

These approaches all assume a knowledge of the value of the point elasticity at its starting position (P_0, Q_0). The line and modified arc elasticities both imply a demand curve along which the point elasticity increases with P, but at a much faster rate in the former case. It stays constant throughout the whole of the arc elasticity curve, and declines as P rises along the midpoint elasticity curve.

These curves are drawn in Fig. 4A.2, on the assumption that the starting point elasticity is -0.3. The choice between the four approaches should be governed primarily by which is likely to give the best approximation to the 'true' demand curve over the range of price changes being considered. [10] To fit in with the general hypothesis stated earlier, this should lie somewhere in between the line and arc approaches. Although the arc and midpoint elasticity curves are close together over the relevant range, the latter can be ruled out as it is further away from the true demand curve for price increases, and is also more complicated.

The modified arc elasticity, which is the only approach that satisfies the general hypothesis completely, must unfortunately be ruled out as well. For although (4A.8) is a relatively straightforward algebraic expression (much more compact than the cumbersome midpoint elasticity formula), it is also too complicated for use as a regular management tool: results of the kind obtained in Appendix 4A.2, for example, cannot easily be derived from it. Hence the choice narrows to the line and arc approaches.

If the modified arc elasticity were a good approximation to the true demand curve, the line elasticity should be chosen as it is much closer to it over the relevant range. However, there is no *a priori* reason why the true demand curve should not be more 'curved' than this and thus much nearer to the arc elasticity approach. (For example, a variation of the modified

Fig. 4A.2   Elasticity demand curves (based on initial point elasticity
$\eta = -0.3$)

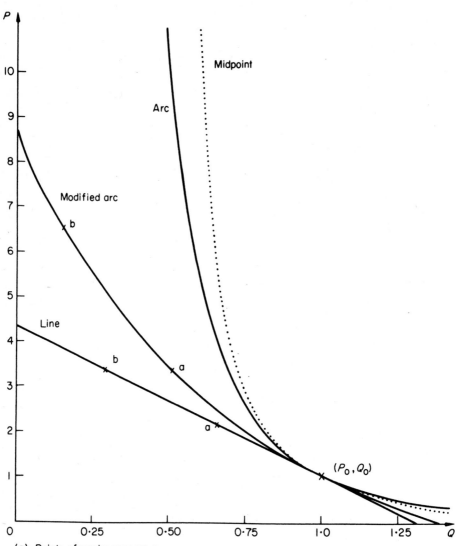

(a) Points of maximum revenue
(b) Points of zero gain in revenue

arc approach which simply doubled the coefficients of p and q in Equation (4A.8) would have that property.)

This underlines the importance of getting good empirical evidence about the response of demand to price changes over the relevant range. Ideally, the actual arc or straight line that is chosen (determined by the value assumed for the initial point elasticity) should depend on which gives the 'best fit' to such empirical evidence. Since we are concerned primarily with price increases, this would (for example) mean rotating the straight line clockwise about the starting point until the 'best fit' was obtained, resulting in the choice of a lower (absolute) initial point elasticity than -0.3. Instead of overestimating passenger losses for all fares increases, this would result in underestimating for small increases and overestimating less wildly for large increases. (There would also, however, be greater underestimates of the growth in demand from fare reductions.) Similarly, the arc elasticity curve would be pulled down and stretched to the left by assuming a higher constant point elasticity. Such a procedure would confirm that the more 'curved' the true demand curve (i.e. the slower the growth in its point elasticity), the more likely it is that the arc elasticity approach is the right one to adopt.

4A.2 Receipts impact of fares increases in an inflationary situation

Let us assume we are considering two consecutive time periods of equal intervals during which the money fare levels for the whole of each period are P_0 and P_1 respectively. There is thus an increase in the money fare level from P_0 to P_1 at the end of the first period and beginning of the second period. If r_0, r_1, are taken as the continuous rates of inflation in each period, then the real price levels at time t are $P_0 e^{-rt}$ during the first period and $P_1 e^{-r_0} e^{-r_1 t}$ during the second period (where t ranges from 0 to 1 in both cases).

Now if Q is the quantity sold per unit of time at time t, and η is the (constant) arc elasticity with respect to the real price level P, then (using a different version of Equation (4A.6) of Appendix 4A.1).

$$Q = a P^{\eta}$$

(where a is a constant). Hence

$$Q = a P_0^{\eta} e^{-\eta r_0 t}$$

during the first period and

$$Q = a P_1^{\eta} e^{-\eta r_0} e^{-\eta r_1 t}$$

during the second period.

To calculate the total receipts obtained in each period, we need to work with the average quantities sold given by

$$\bar{Q} = \int_0^1 Q \, dt$$

Thus

$$\bar{Q}_0 = a \, P_0{}^{\eta} \, \frac{1 - e^{-\eta r_0}}{\eta r_0}$$

$$\bar{Q}_1 = a \, P_1{}^{\eta} \, e^{-\eta r_0} \, \frac{1 - e^{-\eta r_1}}{\eta r_1}$$

The actual proportional increase in receipts (f) between the two periods is given by

$$1 + f = \frac{P_1 \bar{Q}_1}{P_0 \bar{Q}_0}$$

Now since $\dfrac{P_1}{P_0} = 1 + p$, where p is the proportional increase in the money

fare level at the beginning of the second period, it follows that

$$1 + f = e^{-\eta r_0} \, (1+p)^{\eta+1} \, \frac{r_0}{r_1} \cdot \frac{e^{-\eta r_1} - 1}{e^{-\eta r_0} - 1}$$

Since η, r_0 and r_1 will normally be significantly less than one, the quantities ηr_0 and ηr_1 will usually be very small. This means that in most practical calculations it will be appropriate to use a simpler first order approximation to the above equation. And it can be calculated that the following equation is equivalent to the above to the first order in ηr:

$$1 + f = e^{-\eta r} \, (1 + p)^{\eta + 1}$$

Here $r = \frac{1}{2}(r_0 + r_1)$ and is a measure of the average rate of inflation between the two periods. This average can be thought of as the current rate of inflation at the time in the first period that the receipts and fares changes for the second period are being considered. In practical calculations, operators will also normally want to work with annual rates of inflation, rather than the continuous rates assumed in the above calculations. This can be taken into account simply by substituting $1+r$ for e^r in the above equation, giving

$$1 + f = (1 + r)^{-\eta} \, (1 + p)^{\eta + 1}$$

Notes

[1] T.A. Domencich and G. Kraft, *Free Transit,* op.cit.

[2] See, for example, some of the articles collected in R.E. Quandt (ed.), *The Demand for Travel: Theory and Measurement,* Heath Lexington Books, 1970.

[3] M.G. Smith and P.T. McIntosh, *Fares Elasticity: Interpretation and Estimation,* Transport and Road Research Laboratory Supplementary Report 37UC, 1974.

[4] M.H. Fairhurst, *An analysis of factors affecting bus and rail receipts,* London Transport Operational Research Report R201, 1973.

[5] This could be defined by the relationship $1+q = (1+p)^{\eta}$, where q is the proportional change in bus demand resulting from the proportional change p in the bus fare increase relative to the rail fare increase. Thus in this case $q = 0.02$ and $1+p = 1.1/1.2$, so that the cross elasticity works out as -0.23.

[6] See, for example, *Monthly Digest of Statistics,* or *Department of Employment Gazette,* HMSO.

[7] This assumes that inflation during the year will be at the continuous constant rate of $\log(1 + r)$, which is consistent with an annual inflation rate of r.

[8] Greater London Council Minutes 1974, p. 567.

[9] For example, if London Transport's estimate of a £13.9 million gain in bus receipts turned out to be correct, it can be calculated that this implies an elasticity of approximately -0.4 (rather than -0.3). Because of the higher increase in underground fares, however, it might in this case have been better to work with a gross elasticity together with an explicit assumption about cross elasticity, as indicated earlier.

[10] This chapter is concerned with deciding how fares should be increased, rather than reduced. The increases might range up to a doubling of fare values, and the only significant decreases to be considered would be relative reductions in the real price level, up to the inflation rate. Hence a typical range of price changes might be from -20 per cent to $+100$ per cent, or from 0.8 to 2.0 in Fig. 4A.2.

5　Current Practice

The only thing that can be said with any certainty about current practice in fares policy is that we are in the middle of a period of rapid change. News of the latest break with tradition on fares subsidies, or of a change in fare structure or a new special concession, comes almost daily.

Although these changes sometimes occur simply as a result of a different local political representation, they can be seen in a broader context as a reflection of the fundamental underlying changes in public attitudes referred to in the introductory chapter. Thus any snapshot of this rapidly moving situation will be misleading if it fails to indicate the process and direction of change. Hence this chapter attempts to give a broad assessment of underlying trends as well as a reasonably comprehensive picture of the situation in early 1975, considering in turn each of the three categories of fares policy defined on pp. 22–3.

5.1　Fare level

5.1.1　Subsidy requirements

It was noted in Chapter 3 that most public transport operators in Great Britain used to cover their costs largely from fares income, with only modest injections of subsidy mainly on the capital side. But recently the situation has changed, with the most dramatic switch occurring in London. From making an £8 million surplus on current account in 1973, London Transport's operations are now supported by heavy revenue subsidies. In 1974 there was a deficit of £42 million and this had grown to over £100 million in 1975, accounting for more than a third of net working expenses – in spite of the large fares increase implemented in March 1975.[1]

As in other cities, this massive change in subsidy requirements has been caused by a combination of high inflation, a new pay deal for operating staff, and a reluctance to raise fares too readily to meet the escalating costs. But the trend towards greater subsidy began well before the sharp acceleration in inflation rates which developed in 1974. In 1967, for example, some 23 per cent of the public transport operators who were members of the International Union of Public Transport were fully profitable undertakings, in the sense that they covered their total costs (operating costs plus servicing of capital debt) from market income (fares revenue plus receipts from advertising, rent, etc.). But a survey undertaken in 1971 showed this proportion had dropped to 11 per cent by then.[2] Moreover, in 1971 nearly one sixth of operators covered less than half their total costs from market income, while over half of them covered less than three quarters of their total costs in this way. By now it is certain that many operators will have gone even further into the red.

Only one North American city, New York, was included in that part of the survey, and reported that 65 per cent of its total costs were covered by market income. Throughout the United States there has been an accelerating movement towards low fare public transport systems financed by heavy subsidies. Profits from public transport services around the country totalled $66 million in 1950, but total losses approached $200 million in 1970.[3] In these inflationary times holding fares at their current levels would be sufficient to cause major new calls on public funds. But several cities have actually introduced substantial fare reductions in recent years — Los Angeles, San Diego and Atlanta, for example.[4] Thus losses on public transport operations are now likely to be several times greater than they were in 1970. In New York State alone, the Metropolitan Transportation Authority's deficit amounted to over $300 million in 1974.

5.1.2   Overall free fares

Many other towns have introduced free travel in some form or other, but normally as limited special concessions (see later) rather than an overall policy. So far, the only town to have introduced a permanent total free fares policy is Commerce in California. However, although the system has been operating successfully for a long period (since 1962), other towns will find it difficult to draw any useful conclusions from that experience. Commerce is a small, industrial town (10,500 population), and the only public transport is a fleet of five buses operating on three routes connecting the residential areas with the shopping centre. Moreover, the service can be funded from the enormous tax base provided by the large number of corporations working within its boundaries.

Other cities are now considering the possibility of introducing an overall free fares policy. But the only major initiative that has yet been taken was the experiment launched in Rome for the nine days between 30 December 1971 and 7 January 1972, during which no fares were collected in the daytime on all the buses, trams and trolley buses operating within the city's boundaries. (The one underground railway line, and the two suburban rail services to the coastal resorts of Ostia and Alatio, were not involved in the experiment. Night services were also excluded.)

The main fare structure in Rome is a very low flat fare of 50 lire with only half price (25 lire) charged before 8 a.m. Thus fare revenues cover only a small proportion of operating costs — about a quarter at the time of the experiment. The deficit is met entirely by the local government (the Commune), and neither of the two public transport operators have been allowed to increase their fares since 1965. Fare revenues in Rome are now likely to be insufficient to cover the costs of fare collection, and so the introduction of free fares may seem a logical step. However, the experiment seems to have failed in relation to its major objective of reducing car congestion. Although public transport patronage increased by 44 per cent overall compared with the corresponding nine day period the previous year, the increase was only 18 per cent on the one date (7 January) which can be considered as a normal working day, unaffected by public or customary holidays. Surveys suggested that the diversion of car users was small (68 per cent of passengers said they would have used public transport regardless of the experiment). What diversion there was appeared to be mostly for shopping and leisure journeys during the off peak and the increase in passenger traffic was largely made up of children and pensioners.

5.1.3 Organisation and control

A variety of different practices are observed for the organisation and control of the subsidies granted to the public transport operators, and for taking decisions on other aspects of fares policy. Most cities adopt the two tier system (already described in some detail for Great Britain) under which overall policy and financing is the responsibility of a supervising authority, with day-to-day management in the hands of an independent public transport operator. Board members of the operator's organisation are nearly always appointed by the supervising authority whose representatives are in turn sometimes elected directly, and sometimes appointed by the elected city council or by the relevant part of central government.

The most common pattern of organisation is to have just one operator and one controlling authority. But in some cities, particularly those with several styles of public transport service, the situation is more complicated. Paris provides a good example of a complicated organisational structure, with a network of intricate relationships between several central and local government agencies, and the two main public transport operators: the Régie Autonome des Transport Parisiens (RATP), responsible for the Métro, the buses and the Réseau Express Régional (RER) railway; and the Société National des Chemins de Fer Français (SNCF), which operates a substantial network of suburban railway services in Paris. The total revenue subsidies (which amount to about one half of total operating costs) are shared by law in fixed proportions between central government and the various local authorities involved, and controlled through a central agency (the Syndicat des Transports Parisiens) on which they are all represented.

Several cities have set up patterns of organisation with the specific aim of coordinating such diverse interests. Perhaps the forerunner was Hamburg, when in 1965 the eight separate public transport operators (including the German Federal Railway) joined together to form a single 'holding company' (the Hamburger Verkehrsverbund or HVV) with specific overall responsibilities, but allowing each operator to maintain its independence and separate legal status. The HVV is responsible for determining fare levels and structures, and receives all income from fares. It also decides what services should be offered to the public (in terms of routing, frequency, etc.), and 'buys' them from the operators out of the income from fares.

Munich followed with a similar pattern of organisation in 1972. The latest and largest recruit to this way of running things in Germany is the Rhein–Ruhr area. In contrast to Hamburg and Munich where the travel patterns are centred on one large town, the area chosen for the Rhein–Ruhr Verkehrsverbund contains some fourteen cities each of which is an important generator and attractor of traffic in its own right. An office has been set up in Düsseldorf to plan for the setting up of the new association possibly in 1977, when the intention is to bring together some thirty separate public transport undertakings in one organisation.

Perhaps the most comprehensive approach to coordination outside Germany is provided by the Stockholm region, where some ten independent public transport operators were amalgamated in the 1960s into one organisation, Storstockholms Lokaltrafik (SL). SL runs directly all the railway, tram and bus services in the region, except for certain local train services which are operated by the Swedish state railway on contract to SL. The company is responsible to, indeed is owned by, the Greater Stockholm County Council, which was created in 1971 as part of a general reorganisation of local and regional government in Sweden.

Another important example of coordination was the setting up of the Passenger Transport Executives in the British conurbations. There is even talk of a more coordinated approach being adopted for Paris, possibly by giving wider powers and responsibilities to the Syndicat. In London, the main obstacle to a comprehensive coordinated approach to railway planning arises from the distinct and separate responsibilities of London Transport (reporting to the Greater London Council) and British Railways (reporting to the Department of the Environment). Methods of overcoming these difficulties were reviewed in a recent major study of London's railway services.[4] In fares policy the main problem was found to be the rapid divergence between the levels of fares charged by LT and BR, which it was noted could lead to a 'wasteful distortion of traffic patterns'. LT fares remained unchanged between September 1972 and March 1975, whereas there were three separate increases in BR fares in London, making them something like a third higher in January 1975 than they had been at the beginning of the period. This divergence clearly resulted from the two operators being under separate government control. However, having analysed that problem together with a number of other shortcomings in the existing procedures for railway planning and operation in London, the study concluded that they could all be solved without a radical change in organisational structure. The main argument against the creation of a more unified organisation for London seems to be that it would be very difficult to coordinate the policies of the large number of local authorities whose interests would have to be represented on the supervising authority, because of the wide catchment area in south east England from which London commuters are drawn — involving at least another twelve county councils in addition to the Greater London Council.

As far as the financing of the revenue deficits incurred by public transport operators is concerned, there are many different ways in which the necessary funds are obtained. The most common practice is to use the general funds of central or local government, which means that the subsidies come generally from central or local taxation. But in Atlanta and Seattle, for example, the deficits are financed partly by special local sales taxes. And in Paris, the deficit is partly met by the proceeds of an employment tax levied on the Paris region.

5.2 Fare structure

The choice between different fare structures brings home sharply the difficulties of taking decisions in the face of several conflicting objectives. Simplifying the fare structure from a finely graduated scale related to distance at the one extreme, to a flat fare at the other, brings both advantages and disadvantages, which apply particularly to the buses. These are discussed first, together with options towards prepurchase which give rise to similar difficulties. Zonal fares are considered separately, as they bring added advantages (such as the integration of the bus and railway fare systems) but extra difficulties as well.

5.2.1 Structure simplification

In general, the following advantages have been found to apply to the simpler fare structures (the numbers in brackets refer to the objectives listed on pp. 21–2, to which these advantages contribute):

1   The ticketing system is easier for the public to understand and more convenient to use (1(e)).
2   On one man operated buses, they allow for faster transactions with the driver and the installation of simpler and more reliable fare collection and ticket cancelling machinery. This reduces operating costs (3(b)), improves the efficiency of ticketing and fare collection (4(b)), and facilitates the wider extension of one man operation with the resulting amelioration of staffing difficulties (4(c)).
3   They reduce the scope for fare evasion and fraud, because the inspection of passengers' tickets, as well as the checking and handling of ticket stocks and money, is easier (4(d)).

But equally critical disadvantages have also been found (this time the numbers in brackets refer to the objectives that the disadvantages work against):

1   The minimum fare value has to be higher in order to bring in the same amount of revenue. In practice, in order not to impose excessive penalties on the large number of short distance passengers carried by most urban bus undertakings, most systems with bus flat fares have them set at a low level – and this requires substantial revenue subsidies (3(a)).
2   There is a loss of flexibility in adjusting fare levels to meet new revenue targets, and in discriminating between the prices charged to different parts of the market so as to exploit new opportunities for revenue raising or cater for newly identified needs. These problems are reinforced by the fact that simpler fare structures are usually related to single coins in order to bring advantages in simplicity and convenience and the biggest impact on operating costs. If these advantages are to be preserved, it is impossible to provide for marginal increases in revenue, and large and jerky fare increases are needed if and when they come (3(c)).

3 As noted earlier (p. 25), the simpler structures give less of the management information about demand and receipts on individual routes that can be a useful aid to planning and operating the service (4(a)).

Similar advantages and disadvantages follow from the introduction of prepurchase facilities. On their own, they score in being more flexible and less expensive, but lose in making a somewhat lower contribution to improving convenience and reducing operating costs. But it is easier to introduce prepurchase facilities with simpler fare structures. And the introduction of a flat fare in conjunction with a widespread takeup of tickets bought in advance would have the maximum impact on simplicity and convenience for the passenger, and on reducing operating costs.

Nevertheless, such a system would lead to the largest loss of management information and the biggest potential drop in revenue. The extra revenue lost as a result of introducing prepurchase facilities arises because experience shows that they need to be offered at a reasonable discount in order to encourage a worthwhile takeup: yet very few new passengers seem to be attracted by the discount, so that money is virtually being given away to existing passengers who would otherwise have paid a higher cash fare on the bus or at the station.

Many cities round the world, and particularly on the European continent, seem to have come to the view that there is more to be gained than lost by introducing simpler fare structures. More than twice as many cities in 1972 than in 1961 had a flat fare as their only fare structure. This is shown in Table 5.1, which is drawn together from the figures reported for the surveys undertaken in those years of the fare systems adopted by operators who are members of the International Union of Public Transport.[5] Most of the twenty one cities with flat fares as their only fare structure in 1972 are in Western Europe: they include four of the

Table 5.1   Fare structure in cities

	1961		1972	
	Number	%	Number	%
Flat only	8	10	21	23
Graduated only	45	55	23	25
Zonal only	8	10	12	13
Combined	21	26	36	39
All cities	82	100	92	100

Source: See note [5].

twenty two German cities covered by the 1972 survey (Berlin, Bremen, Flensburg, Hagen); three of the nine Swiss cities (Basle, St Gallen, Winterthur); two of the four Spanish (Barcelona and Madrid); and two of the five Italian (Rome and Turin). None of the ten towns in the United Kingdom that were covered by the survey are flat fare cities in that sense. They all have finely graduated fare structures, though three of them (Edinburgh, Liverpool and London) are counted as 'combined' systems in the table as they operate limited flat fare bus services as well. In London, for example, there are eighteen special flat fare bus services operating in the suburbs, and the 'Red Arrow' flat fare bus services which distribute passengers from the main railway termini.

There has also been a significant increase in the use of all forms of prepurchase facility: system passes, multijourney tickets, and season tickets.[6] There is now a widespread use of multijourney tickets in several countries in Western Europe, particularly Belgium, Denmark, France, Germany, Holland and Switzerland. For example, in ten of the twenty two German cities covered by the 1972 survey, more than twice as many passengers used multijourney rather than ordinary single tickets. And although in two of them (Bremen and Hamburg) no multijourney tickets are issued, there is a high takeup of system passes and season tickets instead: the figures in 1972 being 50 per cent and 60 per cent respectively. (The latter figure had risen from 42 per cent only five years earlier.)

There is also an extensive use of system passes in two Swedish cities: Stockholm and Gothenburg. In Stockholm, all existing season tickets were replaced in October 1971 by a monthly system pass allowing for unlimited travel on all Stockholm's public transport services (trains, tubes, trams and buses) during the period of validity of the ticket. Now about 80 per cent of passengers use these system passes, compared with only about a quarter who used the various season tickets that were available before the change. Their high popularity must be due to a large extent to their low price. In early 1975 the price was still at the level at which they had been introduced, namely Skr50 a month. By comparison, charges for single journeys under the zonal fares system (see later) ranged from Skr2 to Skr10 if the tickets were bought for cash and from Skr1,30 to Skr6,50 if multijourney tickets were used. The latter are issued in booklets containing twenty three coupons, and can be bought (along with the system passes) from newspaper kiosks, local agents, enquiry offices and ticket offices.

In the United Kingdom, by contrast, there is as yet very little use of system passes and multijourney tickets, though interest is growing. In June 1972 monthly and annual 'Red Bus' system passes were introduced for London Transport's buses, and their popularity has been increasing. Monthly sales increased from 15,000 in March 1974 to 20,000 by the end of the year, and accounted for some 2·4 per cent of total receipts from bus passengers during the year. As from the fares revision of 23 March 1975, their price was held at the original introductory price of £6 per month and £60 per year, compared with an average increase of 32 per cent in ordinary bus fares; and two new concessions were introduced — free travel for a companion at the weekends, and a special reduced 'add-on' price of £4 per month for underground season ticket holders. Early indications are that all this will have led to a considerable further expansion of sales in 1975 — some 51,000 passes were sold in the first four weeks after 23 March. But at least in relative terms, by far the largest scheme of this kind in Britain is the West Midlands 'Travelcard', introduced in October 1972. This is a system pass valid for weekly or four weekly periods for unlimited travel on virtually all of the bus services operated or controlled by the Passenger Transport Executive. By the end of 1972 some 17,000 Travelcards had been sold, and by the end of May 1975 about 56,000 were in current use, accounting for about 10 per cent of total bus receipts. In July 1975 the scheme was further extended through the introduction of special Travelcards giving holders unlimited travel on specified local railway lines as well.

5.2.2 *Zonal fares*

The previous discussion has compared different types of fare structure in which fares vary according to the distance travelled along a route. Starting with a finely graduated structure, the distance covered by any one fare value can be made greater and greater until in the limit the same fare is charged no matter what the distance travelled — i.e. a flat fare is charged for travel on that route. At first sight it might appear that a zonal fares system combines some of the features of a flat fare and a graduated structure. This is because passengers are charged a flat fare for all local trips that keep within the boundaries of any one zone, while trips crossing zonal boundaries are paid for under what is essentially a graduated fare scale — with the fineness of the scale depending on the number of zones the city has been divided into. However, the flat fare advantages of a zonal fares system are somewhat illusory for travel by the same mode, since similar effects can be achieved just by coarsening the fare scale. The main additional advantages of zonal fares arise if tickets can be used in the same way for travel by any form of public transport, whether bus, trolley bus, tram, train or tube. For each complete journey only one ticket would be needed, and the journey could be made by as many combinations of the different public transport modes that the traveller desired.

The two special advantages that can justifiably be claimed for a comprehensive zonal fares system of that type are the following (the numbers in the brackets refer once again to the relevant objectives in the list of pp. 21–2.

1 Passengers would be free to choose whatever public transport mode suited them best, and use the same ticket (without paying extra) when changing from one vehicle to another both within the same mode (e.g. bus to bus) and between different modes (e.g. bus to train) (1(e)).
2 An improved image for the public transport system as a whole would be created thereby encouraging a greater use of public transport (3(a), 3(e)).

But two special disadvantages also arise:

1 It is no longer possible to charge higher fares on the mode (usually rail) with the lower (in absolute terms) elasticity. Hence, to meet any required revenue target, more passenger miles would be lost than would otherwise have been necessary (3(a)).
2 There are serious problems of ticket issue and control on buses. Drivers or conductors could find it difficult to work out the correct fare for those passengers who did not know which zone their destination was in; and it would be harder for inspectors to check the validity of a passenger's ticket during the journey (4(b), 4(d)).

It is impossible to overcome the first of these disadvantages, whose adverse effects on the maximising revenue objective (3(a)) are likely to be far greater than the offsetting contribution to that objective that would follow from the general improvement to the public transport system's image. The operational difficulties are also formidable, but this time there are methods available to overcome them. For example, the problem of delays in ticket issue on buses could be surmounted by only allowing tickets to be issued beyond the route of the bus to passengers knowing the fare. And fraud evasion could be discouraged by systems of random inspections and spot fines, as practised in some cities on the European continent.

In general, the operational difficulties would be the more acute, the larger the number of zones required and the denser the network. In London, the recent Rail Study observed that 'if the zones were reduced to a number which would be operationally feasible, the fare charged per zone would have to be either so low as to require a heavy subsidy or so high as to result in the loss of a large number of shorter distance passengers. Additionally, zones would be so large that there would be serious anomalies with cross boundary fares.'[7] The study concluded that in spite of its strong attractions, many of the advantages of a zonal fares system could be attained by improving the existing graduated system to which first priority should be given.

Nevertheless, as the earlier table showed, the number of cities operating just zonal fares structures rose from 10 per cent to 13 per cent between 1961 and 1972. And since 1972 at least three more cities have been added to the list. At the beginning of 1973 Gothenburg changed from a graduated fare structure to one based on two main (inner and outer) zones, with tickets valid for travel on all the city's buses and trams. A month later Stockholm changed from a combined system to a zonal structure based on forty three zones: an inner zone surrounded by eleven outer rings, each of which is divided into sectors to form the outer zones.

The zonal tickets in Stockholm are sold as coupons, the charge being two coupons for travel within any one zone and one coupon extra for crossing a zonal boundary. There is a maximum charge of ten coupons. The price of a coupon in early 1975 was Skr1. The booklet of twenty three coupons could be bought for Skr15, making a substantial discount of over a third. The high takeup of system passes mentioned earlier means that only about one fifth of passengers actually make use of the zonal fares system.

The third city to have recently changed over to zonal fares is Frankfurt. There the City Traffic Authority and the German Federal Railway joined together in May 1974 to introduce a new zonal fares system covering all public transport services — the city's trams, buses and underground U-Bahn railway, as well as the Federal S-Bahn railway. The zoning pattern is similar to that in Stockholm. There is one inner zone surrounded by six rings divided into sectors, making forty five zones in all.

In line with the practice in Munich where a similar zonal system is operated, the full advantages of the Frankfurt system can only be obtained by passengers making regular journeys who buy weekly or monthly tickets valid for all travel between defined zones. These tickets are somewhere in between system passes and point-to-point seasons — more flexible than the latter, since they can be used for travel on any public transport service and by any route or line between the chosen zones. The coarser the zonal structure, the nearer these tickets become to system passes. Thus, for example, a ticket bought for zone 1 (the main city and suburbs of Frankfurt) is in effect a system pass for all travel in that zone.

Passengers buying ordinary single tickets have to use a different fare system. This is a very coarse zonal structure, with just four zones. The average fares are much higher than those charged for regular journeys. Thus, for example, single tickets for travel in the inner zone during the rush hour cost DM1 at the time the system was introduced, making over DM40 a month for regular weekday commuters. However, a ticket could be bought under the other system for DM26 a month, valid for all journeys made between Monday and Friday in the inner zone during the month.

The main advantage of confining the full zonal system to regular travellers is that the operational difficulties of ticket issue and control are completely avoided. That point, however, did not affect the rather lukewarm response of the London Rail Study to zonal fares, whose comment on the Frankfurt system was that 'the complications of having two fares systems side by side, the one for season ticket holders and the other for ordinary travellers, are such that we are unable to recommend such a system for London'.[8]

Since then, however, a zonal fares system for regular travellers has also been started in Paris. In July 1975 a new type of ticket was introduced which can be used on the Métro as well as on the buses and the RER and SNCF railways, giving unlimited travel for a month within a defined number of zones. The main fare structures continue as they were before: flat on the Métro, and graduated on the buses and railways. The coarseness of the new zonal structure (there are five concentric zones in all) means that the monthly tickets are very like system passes. Their price was initially set at F40 for travel in one or two zones, and another F20 for each extra zone. The price of a 'carnet' of ten Métro tickets was increased from F8 to F9 at the time the new system was put in.

A more radical innovation in zonal fares is the system planned for the Rhein–Ruhr area when the new transport consortium comes into operation in 1977. Many of the participating undertakings already have zonal fares systems of one kind or another, and they are all to be brought together into what will be the largest integrated zonal fares system in the world, covering an area of over 4,700 square kilometres. The idea is to build the zones at two levels. The smaller zones will be equilateral hexagons, this configuration being chosen as the nearest shape to a circle that will cover an area without leaving gaps. These hexagons, called 'honeycombs', would normally be from between 5 km and 7·5 km in diameter, according to the area covered (a small town or a district within a larger town, for example). The honeycombs are then grouped together into the next charging level of 'circles', which follow administrative boundaries and cover one large town or several smaller areas. Each honeycomb is also to be made the core of its surrounding charging area, thus leading to a greater similarity in fares charged for the same distance travelled in different parts of the network. Compared with other systems which have zones oriented towards one central point, this type is closer to a graduated fare structure and gives extra flexibility in enabling adjustments to be made to the relationship between fares and distance.

5.3 Special concessions

Once the main fare level and structure have been determined, special concessions are concerned with how lower than average prices for special sections of the market can contribute to social and environmental objectives. They can be offered in one or some combination of four main types: within a defined area of the city, for a special service, at a special time of the day or week, or for special groups of people. Examples are described below.

5.3.1 *Special area*

In September 1973 the city of Seattle launched its 'Magic Carpet' service which allowed for free travel on any bus inside an area of 108 blocks covering the central business district. The Magic Carpet area is essentially a free travel zone incorporated within a general 'moving' zonal fares structure. There is a 20 cent charge (with free interchange) for travel in each of the city's other zones, and a further 10 cent charge for crossing all zonal boundaries including that surrounding the Magic Carpet zone. The free travel service replaced a 10 cent 'Dime Shuttle' service that operated in the central business district.

The aims of the Magic Carpet experiment were to increase public transport patronage (which had dropped by more than half over the previous twenty years), to reduce traffic congestion and air pollution, and to conserve energy. A significant contribution to the last two aims was achieved by making adjustments to the regular bus services so that the eight diesel-fueled buses that operated the Dime Shuttle could be completely withdrawn. More generally, it was estimated that the free service led to a 2 per cent drop in traffic volumes, and that this resulted in the carbon monoxide air quality standard being violated on four fewer days each year (it was exceeded on eighty-two days in 1974). It was also estimated that the net annual savings in petrol and diesel oil amounted to some 480,000 gallons. As for patronage, surveys indicated a trebling of bus trips in the central business district (from 4,100 per day before the free service was introduced to 12,300 after it had been operating for nine months) as well as a significant growth in fare paying passengers carried on the rest of the system. About 8 per cent of the trips on the Magic Carpet service had previously been made by car, and a quarter of them would not have been made at all without the service. Some 39 per cent of the trips were for shopping and entertainment, which was consistent with another finding that the free service attracted about $5 million of extra retail sales to the central business district in a year – representing some 1½ per cent of total retail sales in the district in 1973.

The Magic Carpet Service was initially launched as a one year experiment; but extended for another two years (and enlarged to cover another two blocks) when these results were known. It was only a small part of a vigorous and comprehensive plan for improving public transport in Seattle and the surrounding metropolitan county, which was approved in 1972. The plan includes replacing the old and worn out bus fleet; introducing new express bus services connecting the centre of Seattle with the suburbs and improving the local bus services in the suburban communities; putting in special contra—flow bus lanes and extra park-and-ride facilities; and improving bus signs and shelters.

5.3.2 Special service

This category refers to special concessions on a public transport service operating on just one or two special routes or lines. It does not include a special service on the whole or a large part of either the road or the rail network, on the grounds that this would lead to such a large diversion of passengers from the other public transport services as to make it an impracticable proposition.

An interesting example is the Superbus, introduced in Stevenage (a new town in South East England) in March 1971 to connect a residential area (the Chells neighbourhood) on the eastern edge of the town, with the town centre, and the industrial estate on the opposite side to the west. The main aim of the experiment was to encourage car drivers back to the bus for their journey to work, so as to avoid the major highway improvements that would otherwise have been necessary. To achieve these aims the experiment relied entirely on enhancing the attractiveness of the Superbus service, by a combination of fares concessions, improvements in frequency and reliability, and the creation (through the name, a new livery, and special publicity campaigns) of a distinct image as a high quality public transport service. No supporting traffic restraint measures were introduced.

Certain key statistics are given in Table 5.2. The service frequency was more than doubled, and its reliability nearly trebled, during the experiment. When the flat fare was introduced in Phase 3 as a change from the previous graduated fare structure, this meant cheaper journeys for all Chells residents going to the industrial estate and for many of them travelling to the town centre. The major reduction in the flat fare in Phase 5 did, of course, apply to everybody.

Bus patronage more than doubled as a result of these changes. Another remarkable result was that receipts actually increased by more than 50 per cent between May 1971 and July 1973, in spite of the fare reductions during that period: though this would only mean a high (absolute) fares elasticity if the separate influences of the service and image improvements could be shown to have a much smaller impact on demand than the fares concessions. In fact the available evidence seems to indicate that fares reductions had a much more substantial effect on demand than service improvements outside peak hours, but that the situation was quite the other way round with peak period journeys. However, the general increase in the adult fare from 4p to 5p in December 1973 seemed to have had no discernible impact on demand, and thus led to a large further increase in receipts: so that by April 1974 they were nearly double the level in May 1971.

Many of the new Superbus passengers were diverted from their cars: 10 per cent fewer people were driving to work in the areas served by Superbus by the end of the experimental period. Most of the former car drivers appeared from surveys to be using Superbus simply because they preferred it. This suggests that only modest traffic restraint measures would be sufficient to encourage a much greater switch from cars to Superbus.

The only blemish on this highly successful record occurred in early 1975 when service levels could not always be maintained (particularly in peak periods) because of maintenance problems and shortages of spare parts. Problems of that type were common to most British bus operators, partly as a hangover from the three day week caused by the miner's strike at the beginning of 1974, and partly because of the special difficulties that were facing British Leyland and other manufacturers.

Another important example of a special service is the free 'shoppers' bus' introduced in Nottingham (England) as part of a major attack on traffic congestion in the city centre. The service was provided as a counterpart to some radical new traffic restraint measures, so as to enable

Table 5.2

Stevenage Superbus

	Fare	Frequency (average scheduled headway)	Reliability (observed standard deviation from schedule)	Weekly passenger journeys (end of period)	Weekly fare revenue (end of period)
Phase 1 (March–May 1971)	adult: 3–5–7–8–9p child: 2–4–5–6–7p pensioner: half adult fare	12 min.	4·3	20,600	£1,087
Phase 2 (May–July 1971)		7½ min.	1·6	24,900	£1,295
Phase 3 (July–October 1971)	adult: 6p child: 4p			28,500	£1,368
Phase 4 (October 71–February 72)	pensioner: 3p			32,200	£1,622
Phase 5 (February–July 1972)	adult: 4p child: 3p pensioner: 2p	5 min.	1·5	41,000	£1,468
July 1973				45,300	£1,650
December 1973	adult: 5p child: 3p				
April 1974	pensioner: 2p			48,000	£2,050

Source: Stevenage Superbus Experiment — Summary Report.

members of the public to reach the shopping areas from which they had been denied easy access by car. The restraint measures included the elimination of daytime street parking in the city centre and the banning of all through traffic apart from buses. The introduction of some bus lanes gave further assistance to buses, and there was also some street paving in the city centre to aid pedestrians.

There are now two free bus services in operation. The first (Number 88) was introduced in November 1972 to connect the bus stations, car parks and shopping areas, by crossing the city centre in a North—South direction in three main loops. It was put in initially as a three month experiment, but then made permanent. In July 1973 the second service (Number 77) was introduced, crossing the city centre on an East—West axis to connect the General Hospital and other shopping areas not covered by route 88. Both services operate at 5 minute frequencies from between 8 a.m. and 6 p.m. Monday to Saturday. When the special traffic management scheme for banning through traffic was implemented in April 1973, the frequency of route 88 was increased to 4 minutes to cope with the additional demand created at the particularly busy periods of 10.30 a.m. to 4.30 p.m. on Wednesdays, Fridays and Saturdays.

The services are heavily used by the public. Number 88 was carrying around 30,000 passengers a week when it was introduced at the end of 1972, and loadings had increased to some 70,000 a week by the end of 1974. Although route 77 is not nearly as well used (it carries about half the number of passengers), they are both very popular with the public and regarded as a permanent feature of Nottingham's transport system.

5.3.3 *Special time*

A second experiment in free fares on all Rome's buses, trams, and trolley buses was conducted from 2 May 1972 to 30 June 1972. This time, however, the concession was only available from 5 to 8.30 a.m., and 5 to 8 p.m., on Mondays to Saturdays. In addition, over a mile of one of the city's widest and longest thoroughfares (the Via Nomentana) was reserved for bus lanes in both directions. Again, however, the impact of the fares concession was disappointing. Passenger traffic increased by only just over 11 per cent during May compared with the previous year. And 52 per cent of car drivers interviewed at petrol stations said that they would not stop using their cars for any reason. The bus lanes, on the other hand, were highly successful. Along the Via Nomentana lost runs were completely eliminated, the overall speed of the service increased by 10 per cent, and there was a 26 per cent increase in the number of passengers carried.

In Bologna a similar scheme was introduced in April 1973 as a permanent policy. No fares are charged on all the city's public transport services (buses and trolley buses) from up to 9 a.m. in the morning, and 4.30 to 8 p.m. in the evening, on Mondays to Saturdays. Outside these times there is a low flat fare at the same level as in Rome (50 lire). Alternatively, a monthly system pass can be bought from tobacconists or travel agents for 3,000 lire. This is a transferable ticket so can be used by family and friends as well as by the purchaser. The passes are valid at all times of the month (working days and holidays) and on all routes in the network. They were introduced along with the free travel concession to replace the multijourney tickets which could previously be bought in advance; and thereby enabled the administration to simplify the service and dispense with all ticket cancelling machinery on one man buses. The new fares policy was put in as part of a general plan for restricting car traffic and increasing public transport usage, which included widespread parking restrictions and extensive bus priority measures. Although no solid information is available about the success of the policy, the administration appears to be happy with the results so far.

A third Italian city, Prato, introduced free fares during restricted periods in October 1972. In all three cities, the free travel concession is limited mainly to the rush hours in order to have the maximum impact on the environmental objective of reducing traffic congestion. (The exception is that the concessions in Rome and Bologna are available right from the beginning of the day, when traffic is light. This implies a subsidiary social objective as well: namely to improve the lot of the lower paid workers who have to get to work early in the morning.) It should be noted that this approach is in conflict (but for good reasons) with the standard economic approach to pricing policy: that higher charges should be made at peak times (related to the higher marginal costs of providing the service at those times), in order to maximise revenue and bring demand more closely into line with supply.

5.3.4 *Special group*

In Bologna free travel is also available as a special concession to students attending schools and colleges during term time. On the production of an identity pass, they can travel free from between 12 noon and 3 p.m., or from 8 p.m. to the end of the day if they are attending evening classes.

This is an illustration of a fairly common practice to make travel concessions available for special groups of people in off peak periods. Free or low fares for old people and children outside peak hours is a common phenomenon, and special concessionary tickets for family groups travelling together are becoming more popular.

Concessionary fares for children do, of course, stem from the long-standing tradition to offer them special tickets often priced at half the adult fare. Free or low fares for old people are a more recent phenomenon, but now a widespread practice in a large number of towns in Europe and North America.

Further discussion of these points is left to the next chapter, where the practice in London is described in some detail.

5.4 Lessons from experience

On fare levels, it is difficult to draw any general conclusions from the vigorous movement towards higher subsidies which has been noted, since it is too early to judge how that powerful trend will be affected by the harsher economic climate that now faces many industrialised cities. The same applies to fare structures, since the equally powerful trend towards the simplest structure (the flat fare) has only been possible because of the willingness of many urban governments to accept much higher subsidy levels.

The broad alternatives in the future would seem to be either to hold fares and thereby move fairly quickly towards a situation in which public transport becomes a free or heavily subsidised social service, financed almost entirely from central or local taxation; or to accept regular fare increases to keep up at least partly with inflation as a normal fact of life, even though this may still mean increasing the money level of the subsidy each year. In either event increasing interest in the development of new and buoyant forms of local taxation to meet the mounting deficits may become apparent.

If regular fare increases are decided upon, this might cause the flat fare, with its lack of flexibility in adusting to meet new revenue targets, to become less popular: with perhaps a switch back to coarsely graduated fare structures (so as to retain at least some of the advantages of structure simplification), or an accelerating movement towards zonal fares.

The recent interest in zonal fares may also have reflected the trend towards more integrated organisational structures. For it is undoubtedly easier to implement the same zonal fares structure for all the city's public transport services if they are all controlled by the one unified organis-ation. Experience has confirmed that this is so, as most of the towns with zonal fares have (or plan to have) a single overall organisation for public transport as well — Hamburg, Frankfurt, Munich, Stockholm, and the Rhein—Ruhr area, for example. Hence if the trend towards integrated organisational structures continues (as seems likely), there may also be a continued growth in the implementation of integrated zonal fare structures.

Finally, it is important to note that the first Roman experiment in the blanket application of free fares was implemented on its own without any supporting transport policies, and failed completely in meeting its stated objectives. The second experiment fared little better, with the only success arising from the one supporting measure (the bus lane) rather than from the free travel concession. By contrast the free fares policies in Seattle and Nottingham, for example, were both introduced as just one component of a broader transport strategy, and were thereby much more successful. These and other examples suggest what is perhaps the most important lesson to be drawn from past experience: that fares policies will be much more effective if conceived as an integral part of a total transport strategy, and implemented along with complementary service improvements, traffic restraint measures, and so on.

Notes

[1] These surplus and deficit figures refer to the difference between market income and operating costs, and do not make any allowance for depreciation and renewal of capital.

[2] E. Ellen and I. Phillips, *The financing of capital and revenue costs of public transport undertakings,* UITP, 40th International Congress, 1973.

[3] P. Gapp, 'Modern Transit', *Metropolitan,* March/April 1974.

[4] *London Rail Study,* Part II, Chapter 18, GLC 1975.

[5] R. Gutnecht, *Alternative approaches to public transport fares with their revenue and traffic implications,* UITP, 40th International Congress, 1973.

[6] These are defined on p. 21.

[7] See *London Rail Study,* op.cit., p. 100.

[8] Ibid., p. 100.

6 Social Implications

6.1 Introduction

Of the five social objectives listed on p. 21, the last three are influenced only indirectly by fares changes via their impact on the quality of service. Such improvements in service quality would be achieved mainly through changes in fare structure, as discussed earlier. This chapter considers the impact of fares changes on the first two of the social objectives, namely on income redistribution and on improving travel opportunities for specific social groups.

Here the implications of fares policy decisions are important for three main reasons. First, most government bodies, of whatever political complexion, tend to consider these two objectives as a vital part of their strategies for public sector provision. Secondly, all fares policy decisions – whether they involve changes in fare structure, fare level, or the introduction of special concessions – will have an impact on these objectives. Thirdly, these impacts will be a direct result of the fares decision and be felt immediately by all the individuals concerned. It is therefore necessary to determine the nature and extent of these effects as carefully as possible, so that local councillors can get a better understanding of the direct implications of their decisions for different sorts of people.

Much of the analysis in this chapter concerns travel behaviour in London, using information from two surveys – the Family Expenditure Survey (FES) for 1972[1] and the Greater London Transportation Survey (GLTS) 1971–72.[2] The two surveys are not strictly comparable, the main differences being in sample size (GLTS has over 40,000 households whereas FES in London has only 850), and in the fact that their classifications for income bands are not quite the same. However, these differences are not significant enough to cast any serious doubt on the conclusions drawn.

6.2 Income distribution

Dealing first with income distribution, the key issue is the extent to which a policy decision involving a higher subsidy from central or local taxes would tend to transfer income from richer to poorer households, or vice versa. Policy makers also need a working rule to judge the cut off point at which these transfers change from being desirable to undesirable.

For this purpose it is appropriate to use the commonly accepted definition that a policy change is progressive, neutral, or regressive, according to whether poor people gain more, stay the same, or lose more than rich people, when these gains or losses are expressed not as absolute sums, but as proportions of disposable income (gross income, plus refunds, less taxes). This recognises that an extra £1 of net income will be worth more to a less well off person; but as a working rule it must be used with care, for it also implies the particular assumption that this marginal extra benefit is inversely proportional to the level of disposable income. (It means, for example, that a poor man earning one tenth as much as a rich man will derive ten times the benefit from the same increase in his net income.)

Clearly a high subsidy policy will be the more progressive the more the subsidies are found from a progressive source of funds like income tax, and the less from a regressive source like (for example) a sales tax which bears equally on all who buy the goods in question, regardless of their income. British local property taxes (rates) are a good example of a source of subsidy somewhere in between those two extremes. Poorer households not only tend to pay less rates than richer, but can get refunded for some of the rates they pay under the rate rebate scheme. Although these refunds come initially from local government the local councils get reimbursed by central government for what they pay back to ratepayers under the scheme. The amount of refund depends on family structure as well as household income.

Even after rate rebates have been taken into account, it has been correctly observed that rates are still a regressive form of taxation.[3] However, it does not necessarily follow that a switch in policy towards paying for public transport out of rates rather than fares has adverse effects on income distribution — mainly because higher fares can be regressive as well.

In order to explore this issue a detailed analysis is given in Appendix 6A.1 of the effects of different policies towards fare and rate levels in London. In interpreting these results it should be recognised that except for the rebates that are given, rates are taxes on property rather than on individuals; and that higher public transport fares must normally be paid in the same way by all who use the services regardless of their income. Hence the analysis has to be concerned with average transfers of income between groups of people at different levels of income, rather than actual transfers between individuals; bearing in mind that although richer people on average spend more on rates and fares than poorer people, this does not necessarily apply to each individual.

British Railways' fares are not included in this part of the analysis since they are outside the control of the authority responsible for choosing between higher fares and higher rates, namely the Greater London Council. The general problems of separate control were touched on briefly in Chapter 5. A social dilemma would arise if BR suburban fares continued to rise at a faster rate than underground fares, as they have done in recent years. For this would, for example, mean that ratepayers in south London, who have to rely mainly on BR services for railway travel, would be subsidising those living north of the river who would be paying much lower fares on their extensive network of underground services. Apart from that point, however, the conclusions drawn in this section apply broadly to changes in BR suburban as well as underground fares, since the income distributions of people using these two types of railway service are broadly similar.

The amount spent on bus fares, underground fares and rates by London households is greater the higher the household's income, the biggest differences arising with underground fares. When expressed as a proportion of mean disposable income, however, expenditure on both bus fares and rates is lower at higher incomes, while with underground fares it stays at about the same level (see Table 6.1). This confirms that although rates are indeed regressive as far as different income groups are concerned, higher bus fares are regressive in their impact as well. Higher underground fares, on the other hand, seem on average to be marginally progressive.

Table 6.1

Mean household expenditure on fares and rates as percentage of mean disposable income (Greater London, 1971−72)

	Gross weekly household income			
	£0−30	£30−60	£60+	All households
Bus	1·7	1·2	0·7	1·0
Underground	1·1	1·1	1·2	1·2
Bus and underground	2·8	2·3	1·8	2·1
Rates				
before rebates	7·4	3·8	2·6	3·5
after rebates	6·9	3·8	2·6	3·5

Source: GLTS 1971−72 (bus and underground fares), FES 1972 (rates).

There are also four other factors which have an important influence on how different fare and rate levels affect income distribution in any British city:

1 The proportion of the local government's rate income that comes from domestic households, rather than from commercial, industrial and other undertakings.

2 The proportion of the public transport operator's fares income that comes from nonresidents (i.e. from people who do not pay the local rates – principally tourists and commuters across the city's boundary).

3 The amount of refund that can be obtained from central government in rate rebates.

4 The way in which the increased rates borne by non-domestic concerns are passed on in higher prices.

The analysis in Appendix 6A.1 shows what would happen under a switch from a hypothetical policy based on relatively high fares for London Transport's bus and underground services with comparatively little contribution from the rates; to one based on lower fares and a higher rate contribution, with no assistance from central government except in rate rebates. Using available estimates for the first two of the above factors and making reasonable assumptions about the other two; and assuming further that the fares changes apply in the same proportion to both buses and underground; then it appears that the average London household would gain from a high rate rather than a high fare policy, regardless of income. When these gains are expressed as proportions of disposable income, it seems that a high rate policy would be regressive – but only marginally so. In fact it would not take much to tip the balance; and it might be enough just to keep bus fares lower than underground fares, or to obtain additional revenue grant from central government, to make a low fares policy progressive. More specifically, it appears that if it were possible to change from a high to a low fares policy confined just to the buses, this would be progressive even if financed entirely from the rates.

Although these conclusions are based on an analysis of the situation in London, they may be more generally applicable. This can be seen first from Figure 6.1, which shows that household expenditure on bus fares by different income groups follows a similar pattern in Greater London as in the rest of the United Kingdom. Moreover, although in London expenditure on railway fares is (not surprisingly) much greater and there is a wider variation between the lower income groups in the amounts they spend, the gap between the highest income groups is roughly the same as elsewhere in the country. We would also expect the relationship between

Fig. 6.1   Household expenditure on bus, coach and railway fares (United Kingdom 1972)

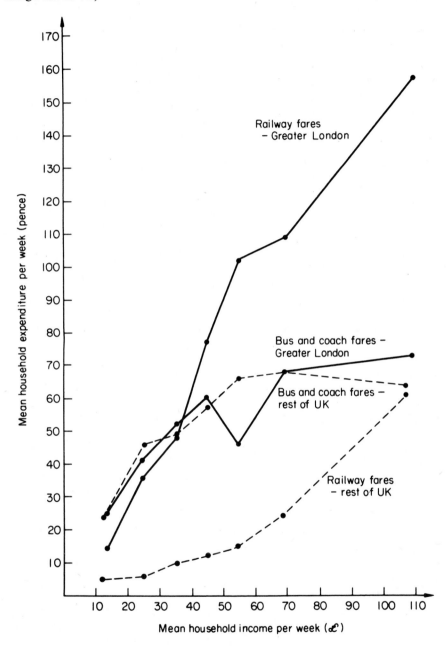

Source: Department of Employment.

rates expenditure and income to be broadly similar in different parts of the country. As for the four other influences noted above, there is not likely to be much difference between London and other British cities in either 1, 3, or 4. The value of 2, however, will be considerably lower in other towns, since London has a much higher proportion of visitors and commuters across its boundary, and this has the effect of making a low fare policy more progressive outside London.

Hence it appears that the most progressive fares policy initiative that could be taken in cities with the bus as the predominant form of public transport (which applies to all towns in the United Kingdom apart from London) would be to introduce a general policy of free bus travel, even if this had to be financed entirely from the rates.

More generally, it seems that to make the maximum contribution to the income redistribution objective, the costs of public transport services should be met by increasing 'prices' in the following order of priority. Firstly, raise income tax and pay for the costs of running public transport through a central government grant. Secondly, increase railway fares. Thirdly, increase rates so as to finance any remaining deficit on public transport operations from a local government grant. And finally, if still more money is needed, get it in the last resort by increasing bus fares.

It may well be that this order of priority — income tax, railway fares, local property taxes, bus fares — is applicable to industrialised cities outside the United Kingdom as well, since one might expect to find a reasonably common relative distribution of expenditure on these four items as between different income groups. But the policy could only be followed precisely on those lines in towns with comparatively small suburban railway networks which do not excessively duplicate either the journey purposes or the routes served by the bus network. For in a town like London with a substantial network of both rail and bus services, such a policy would cause fares to diverge too widely, which would be likely to result in excessive diversion of passengers from trains to buses thus creating discomfort and inconvenience and unmanageable bus operating problems. In these circumstances, the following would appear to be the right order of priority in terms of making the greatest contribution to the redistribution of income from rich to poor: firstly, finance public transport to the maximum feasible extent from central government grant; next, raise both rail and bus fares, but the former by a greater amount so as to create the greatest feasible differential between them; and finally, finance any remaining deficit from local government grant.

This means that the decision by central government to make a large grant in 1975–76 to meet the revenue deficits of the bus and underground operations financed by the English county councils (see p. 55) appears also to have made a substantial contribution to the income redistribution objective. (In London, the grant amounted to £53 million towards a forecast revenue deficit of £112 million in 1975—76).[4] By the same token, the government's stated intention to reduce the real value of its revenue grants in future years implies a regressive approach to income distribution, and will need to be justified either by a denial of that particular objective, or on the grounds that such a policy will achieve more important gains against others.

These conclusions, however, must be treated with caution for several reasons. Firstly, the calculations in Appendix 6.1 have made questionable assumptions about the amounts that are obtained in rate rebates and the way in which higher rates are passed on in higher prices (3 and 4, above), and more reliable estimates of these two parameters are sorely needed. This is important for central as well as local government, because of the remarks made earlier (p. 45) about the need to ensure that its policies for national income distribution are adequately fulfilled. Thus the amount given in rate rebates affects the extent to which local taxes are progressive (though it should be borne in mind here that the increasing unpopularity of rates is reinforcing pressures for new forms of local taxation which are likely to be brought to a head when the Layfield Committee, which was set up by the government in 1974 to 'review the whole system of local government finance in England, Wales and Scotland', reports its findings). Furthermore, the way in which higher rates are passed on in higher prices both within and without any local county council's area of responsibility will influence the distribution of income both within and between counties; and central government should ideally be in a position to ensure that such transfers of income are consistent with national policy aims. Secondly, it should be noted that the calculations have depended on the relative expenditures on rates and fares of different income groups at one point in time (1971—72), and have made no allowance for the fact that the relevant ratios may change independently through time. Thus, for example, expenditure on rates was higher in inner than in outer London in 1971—72, but the situation was the other way round the following year, and indeed had been in most of the preceding years, perhaps implying that rates in London are usually more progressive than indicated in this analysis, in view of the lower average incomes in inner London. Thirdly, the true impact of special forms of assistance like rate rebates may depend on the problems of identification and social stigma that tend to bedevil adequate social service provision (see p. 40 above). And finally, it must be recalled that although poor people on average, when treated as a group, may be better off as a result of a low fares policy, some of them would be much worse off — if they live in houses with high rateable values, or do not use public transport at all, for example. This last point makes it essential to look at these problems from different angles so as to get a better feeling for the full social impact of fares policies.

6.3 Travel behaviour and household income

Households might respond to increases in their real income (whether resulting from an effective reduction in real fare levels, or otherwise) either by travelling further by public transport, or more frequently, or both. To consider such effects the mean fare per trip, available from the GLTS, can be used as a proxy for trip length; and comparisons can be made with the number of trips undertaken (i.e. the trip rate).

Statistical analyses of how average fares paid and numbers of trips made by London households change according to income are carried out in Appendix 6A.2 for both bus and rail travel, taking account of the separate influences of the number of people in the household and whether a car is owned. The analysis brings out the way in which travel behaviour responds to marginal variations in income; using the concept of point income elasticity defined (loosely speaking) as the ratio of a small proportional change in trip rate (or another variable) to the small proportional change in income that has caused it.[5] Normally we would expect that at higher income levels changes in income will have less effect on the use people make of public transport, i.e. that point elasticities will decline as income rises; and this is borne out by the statistical analysis except in the case of trip lengths on the railways. These and other findings are summarised below.

6.3.1 *Bus trips*

Figure 6.2 indicates how mean household expenditure, fare per trip and trip rate for bus travel vary with gross median household income, with the means and median calculated for the ten income bands by which the GLTS data are classified. The chart shows that the higher a household's income, the more it is likely to spend on bus fares — except in the highest income bracket (median income £6,000 per annum in 1971—72) where the expenditure is relatively lower. This is a result of people in the highest income group using buses less frequently. But the length of the bus journeys which people make does not differ very much between income

112

Fig. 6.2　Daily bus trips and bus fares expenditure (means per household, Greater London, 1971–72)

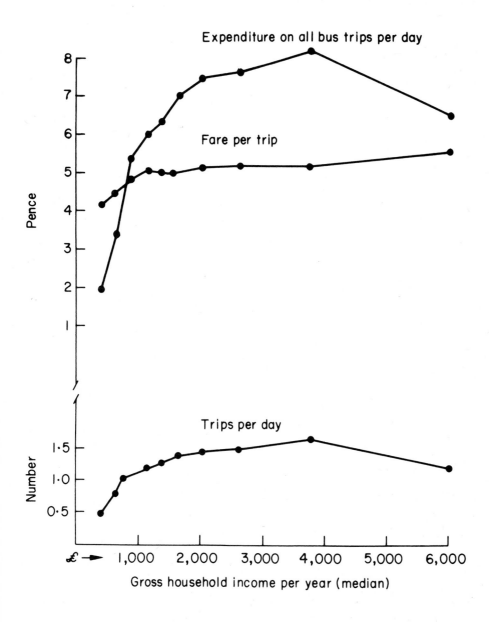

groups, and only in the lower income brackets do households with smaller incomes make significantly shorter journeys.

Table 6.2 shows the point elasticities calculated from Equations (6A.12) and (6A.13) for a range of household incomes. At lower incomes the effect of changes in income on bus fares expenditure is very large (with the point elasticity greater than one for the lowest income group); and this is accounted for much more by changes in the numbers of trips made than in fare per trip (or trip length). Increases in the number of trips taken account for over 70 per cent of the total increase in expenditure for all incomes of up to £1,375 per annum, which cover over a third of all households in the GLTS sample. However, although the trip rate elasticity starts off at a high level, it declines quickly; whereas the fare per trip elasticity starts off at a much lower level but declines slowly. At the median income for all households in GLTS (£1,750 per annum), both elasticities are at a very low level and nearly equal. The trip rate elasticity begins to dominate again when it becomes negative at above £2,000 per annum. Thus households appear to respond to increases in their income by hardly changing the length of their bus trips. Instead, they tend to respond by going out on the buses much more often than before if they are poor and less than before if they are rich.

6.3.2   Rail trips

In some ways it might seem desirable to carry out similar analyses for London's railway services separately for the two distinct groups into which they are divided. For the British Rail suburban services, unlike the London Transport underground, operate to a timetable; cover longer distances on average and have wider gaps between stations; and have a different (more finely graduated) fare structure. However, the British Rail and London Transport services are much closer to each other in all these respects than they are to the bus services. There is also a much sharper distinction between the railway services as a whole, catering for comparatively fast, reliable journeys between fixed points on the network, and the bus services which provide for slower and less predictable journeys, but which enable more varied and flexible travelling patterns. Moreover, the previous bus analysis, which covered the whole of London, can only be truly compared with a corresponding rail analysis taking the railways together as a group. For otherwise there would be a distorted geographical coverage, arising from the point made earlier that south London is very poorly served by the underground but has an extensive network of British Rail suburban services, while the situation is quite the other way round in

Table 6.2

Elasticities of bus trips and bus fares expenditure, with respect to gross household income

	Gross household income per year (£)										
	400	625	875	1,125	1,375	1,625	1,750*	2,000	2,600	3,750	6,000
Elasticities with respect to gross household income of:											
1 number of trips (T)	0·79	0·58	0·41	0·29	0·19	0·11	0·08	0·01	−0·12	−0·30	−0·52
2 fare per trip (L)	0·23	0·16	0·12	0·10	0·08	0·07	0·07	0·06	0·05	0·04	0·03
3 expenditure on all bus trips (F) (1 + 2)	1·02	0·74	0·53	0·39	0·27	0·18	0·15	0·07	−0·07	−0·26	−0·49

Source: Appendix 6A.2, Equations (6A.12) and (6A.13) in unrounded form (coefficients to five places of decimals, not shown in text).

*This is the median income of all households in GLTS. The other columns are the median incomes of the ten income bands into which the GLTS data are classified.

north London. For these reasons the following analysis covers all London's railway services together as one group.

Urban railways are used primarily as mass carriers of people to and from work in the morning and evening peaks, and for this reason alone we would expect somewhat different relationships to apply than those found in the previous analysis of bus travel. (According to GLTS, 77 per cent of all journeys by British Rail made by London residents are to and from work, compared with 62 per cent of all underground journeys, and only 42 per cent of bus journeys.) However, the fact that most rail commuters use season tickets or returns for their journeys prevents a strictly comparable analysis from being carried out. This is mainly because the variety of different discounts offered by BR and LT makes it very difficult to define the 'fares per trip' paid by the holders of such tickets in a way which is a comparable reflection of the lengths of the trips undertaken by ordinary single ticket holders. Hence the following analysis is confined to holders of ordinary single tickets when fare per trip is being considered.

Figure 6.3 shows that rail trip rates in London increase with income. Unlike the case with bus travel, however, there is no sign of 'turn down' at the higher income levels. This is true of both season and ordinary single ticket holders, though trips made on season tickets account for an increasingly higher proportion of all rail trips by London households as their income increases. Some 61 per cent of all rail trips are made with season or return tickets, with the proportions rising from 44 per cent in the lowest income group to 65 per cent in the top income group. Car owning households also make greater use of season and return tickets, at all income levels. Some 66 per cent of all rail trips by car owning households are made in this way, compared with the corresponding figure of 56 per cent for households without cars.

Figure 6.3 also shows how the fares paid on trips with ordinary single tickets vary with income. An important point brought out by Appendix 6A.2 is that the trip length elasticity for such ticket holders tends to increase in response to growth in income for the majority of households, whereas it declines for bus travel for virtually all households. This result is not at all implausible, and could be interpreted by an hypothesis that as their income grows, people tend to take the opportunity of making the longer rail journeys that they can now afford, and of living further away from where they work. However, the trip length elasticity reaches a maximum at a level of household income not much greater than the median for all households, and thereafter follows the more common pattern of declining elasticity with growing income.

116

Fig. 6.3 Daily rail trips and fares per trip, by ticket type (means per household, Greater London 1971–72)

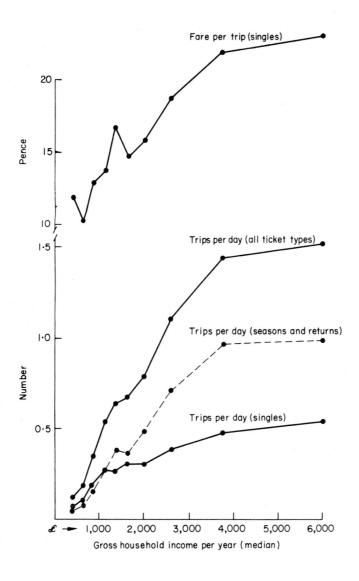

Table 6.3 shows the point elasticities calculated from Equations (6A.15) and (6A.16) for the same range of incomes shown in Table 6.2. This time the response at lower income levels is even greater, with the trip rate elasticity alone as high at 1·21 for the lowest income group. Moreover, although the trip rate and trip length elasticities are no longer strictly comparable, changes in trip rate account for nearly all the response to income changes at the lower income levels if we adopt the reasonable assumption that the trip length elasticities of season and single ticket holders follow a broadly similar pattern. However, with trip rate elasticity falling, and fare per trip elasticity initially rising, there comes a point at which the two are equal — which could be reached at an income of about £1,600 a year. For households with higher incomes than this (which account for just over a half of all households) changes in trip length rather than trip rate become the dominant influence. Thus although the poorer households appear to respond to increases in their income by travelling more frequently by rail, but hardly changing the length of their trips, the response seems to be quite the other way round with the richer households.

6.3.3 Conclusions

Four important conclusions can be drawn from this section. First, richer passengers do not on average make significantly longer bus journeys, thus refuting what has hitherto been a commonly accepted view about travel behaviour. This suggests that a change from a graduated to a flat bus fare structure is not necessarily regressive. Thus, for example, if London Transport's March 1975 fares revision had involved a complete switch to a 5p flat bus fare, it would have conferred considerable benefits on long distance passengers, but involved a sharp rise (of 67 per cent) for those making 3p journeys which accounted for a significant proportion (some 40 per cent) of all bus journeys in London. But all income groups would have benefited on average by similar amounts, the 5p fare being somewhat lower than the average fare paid before the change, with no significant difference between people of different incomes.

Secondly, the extra expenditure on both bus and railway fares incurred by poorer households as their income rises is accounted for largely by the extra number of trips they make, rather than by the length of those trips.

Thirdly, the increases in the number of trips made by poorer households in response to rising incomes appear to be very large. This point is particularly significant if it can be assumed that increases in income have a similar impact to reductions in fares (an assumption which is supported by

Table 6.3

Elasticities of rail trips and rail fares expenditure, with respect to gross household income

	Gross household income per year (£)												
	400	625	875	1,125	1,375	1,625	1,750*	2,000	2,600	3,750	6,000		

Elasticities with respect to gross household income of:

1 number of trips *(T)*, all ticket types

| | | 1·21 | 0·78 | 0·55 | 0·43 | 0·35 | 0·30 | 0·28 | 0·24 | 0·19 | 0·13 | 0·08 |

2 fare per trip *(L)*, ordinary single tickets only

| | | 0·17 | 0·22 | 0·26 | 0·29 | 0·31 | 0·32 | 0·32 | 0·32 | 0·32 | 0·30 | 0·25 |

Source: Appendix 6A.2, equations (6A.15) and (6A.16).
*See note to Table 6.2.

119

the evidence discussed later about the large response by London's old age pensioners, with lower than average incomes, to the free off peak bus fares introduced in September 1973). For if this were so the fact that the total bus and rail expenditure elasticities with respect to income have been estimated at greater than one for the poorest income group, means that a reduction in public transport fares would lead to an increase in fares revenue if these concessions could be limited to that group of people. And the impact of reductions in bus fares on households without cars would be even greater, since they seem to have even higher income elasticities (see later).

Fourthly, however, richer households appear to respond to income changes in a different way than poorer, particularly with regard to bus travel. Above a certain income level, households will spend less on bus travel as their income increases: which implies that at some stage the bus becomes an 'inferior' good, which the householder gives up for something better. A somewhat exaggerated picture of how such a change might work out in practice would be provided by the family which moves out to a high class suburb in response to an increase in income, with the husband changing from the bus to the train for work journeys, and the wife and children giving up the bus for the car for all shopping, school and leisure journeys.

6.4 Implications for social groups

Apart from income, there are several other important influences on people's reactions to different fares policies: such as whether they own a car or have one available for their journey, their social class, occupation, age and sex. Many of these factors are, of course, closely interrelated. Thus poorer people are likely to be disadvantaged in other ways as well: to be without a car, working class, unemployed, or older, for example. This makes it difficult to disentangle from available data the separate influence on travel behaviour of other aspects of social structure, apart from income. Nevertheless, it is vital to make some attempt at clarifying these issues. For otherwise policy makers would be unable to judge whether a fares policy aimed, say, at selectively increasing the real income of poor people, by reducing their fares, would be sufficient to outweigh the other disadvantages from which they suffer.

6.4.1 *Car ownership*

A close association between income and car ownership is to be expected. The strength of this association is indicated by GLTS data, which show that only 6 per cent of London households with less than £500 a year in

1971–72 owned a car, but that this proportion rose to 88 per cent for those earning more than £5,000 a year. The FES reveals a similar pattern. In 1972 just over 2 per cent of households in the UK earning less than £10 per week owned a car, rising to 89 per cent of those whose incomes were greater than £80 a week.

Appendix 6A.2, however, shows that owning a car has a similar effect on bus and rail trip rates at all income levels, in that it leads to the same substantial proportionate reduction in the number of trips made regardless of income or household size. Table 6.4 shows that car ownership causes a much larger reduction in bus trips, as one would expect; but it has a substantial effect on rail trips as well. London households with two or more cars make a third as many bus trips, and half as many rail trips, as carless households; and even households with just one car still make only half as many bus trips. Regardless of household size, car ownership thus appears to have a much more substantial effect on trip making than does the level of household income.

Table 6.4

Reduction in trip rate arising from car ownership
(Greater London, 1971–72)

	Reduction in number of	
	bus trips (%)	rail trips (%)
Households owning:		
one car	−53	−39
two or more cars	−67	−50

Source: Appendix 6A.2, Equations (6A.12) and (6A.13).

As for trip length, Appendix 6A.2 shows that ownership of a car has no significant effect for railway travel, and little impact as far as the buses are concerned other than to reduce still further the already small variation between households of different incomes. And while the low income householder is more likely to make longer bus journeys as his income increases, it is only if he does not own a car that he will do so to any noticeable extent (the elasticities of households without cars being significantly higher at all income levels).

Bus travel is also heavily influenced by whether a car is actually available for the journey being taken, regardless of ownership. GLTS data show that although 53 per cent of all London households owned a car in

1971–72, some 95 per cent of all bus passengers did not have one available for their journey (with the proportion still as high as 90 per cent for passengers with more than £5,000 a year). This implies that in spite of rising car ownership, the social factors limiting car availability mean that nearly all bus passengers are still dependent on the bus as their only form of transport.[6]

6.4.2 *Social class*

It is useful to compare the pattern of travel behaviour outlined in the last section with the social class of the household. Table 6.5 shows that a high proportion (some 43 per cent) of the heads of the poorest London households (who in response to increases in real income potentially generate a large increase in public transport trips) are economically inactive. Although this category does not include those registered as unemployed, this high proportion might nevertheless suggest that the provision of extra job opportunities in London would have the important incidental effect of increasing bus and rail travel and hence London Transport's revenue. By contrast, the higher income groups are dominated by middle class professionals, who are already 'saturated' with bus travel.

Table 6.5

Socio-economic group of household head: by gross household income
(Greater London, 1971–72)

	Gross household income (£ per year, %)					All incomes
	0–749	750–1499	1500–2999	3000–4999	5000+	
Employers, managers professional workers	3	7	17	40	67	18
Intermediate nonmanual	3	6	10	13	12	8
Junior nonmanual	9	20	16	13	8	15
Foremen and supervisors	3	7	12	9	3	9
Skilled manual	11	21	26	14	4	20
Semiskilled manual	12	17	10	5	2	11
Unskilled manual	7	8	5	2	1	5
Economically inactive	43	9	3	2	2	10
Occupation inadequately described	10	5	2	2	2	4
All households	100	100	100	100	100	100
Expanded sample nos. ('000 = 100%)	450	698	1244	420	139	2950

Source: GLTS.

6.4.3 Occupation

Turning now to London's bus passengers rather than the households from which they come, Table 6.6 shows that over a quarter (27 per cent) of the trips made by the poorest income group are by retired people. The dominance of housewives in the low rather than high income groups is presumably a reflection of the fact that richer housewives use the car rather than the bus for shopping and taking the children to school.

Table 6.6

Trips made by bus passengers: by gross household income and occupation (Greater London, 1971—72)

	Gross household income (£ per year, %)					All incomes
	0—749	750—1499	1500—2999	3000—4999	5000+	
Working fulltime	10	50	58	65	59	54
Working parttime	16	13	14	9	6	12
Unemployed	2	1	1	1	1	1
Retired	27	6	1	1	1	4
Housewife	37	16	10	7	9	13
Student	6	13	17	18	24	16
Other	2	1	—	—	1	—
All bus trips	100	100	100	100	100	100
Expanded sample nos. ('000 = 100%)	278	832	1804	682	169	3765

Source: GLTS.

The Family Expenditure Survey gives an interestingly different slant on the occupations of bus (as compared with rail) travellers. Table 6.7 shows that households in the United Kingdom headed by manual workers spend far more than any other group on bus and coach fares, whereas with railway fares the situation is reversed — with those in professional and administrative occupations spending four times as much as manual workers. Moreover, it would appear that only 13 per cent of manual workers' households used the railways at all, compared with 30 per cent of the professional and administrative households. The dominance of bus travel in households headed by retired people is even more striking. Only 6 per cent of them made use of the railways, compared with 57 per cent for the buses; and those who travelled by train did not seem to do so very often, spending only a quarter as much on fares as those who travelled by bus. This is probably because retired people mostly go out on local trips, and use the bus for this purpose as it is the most suitable form of public transport for short distances.

123

Table 6.7

Household expenditure on fares: by occupation of household head
(United Kingdom, 1973)

	Railway fares		Bus and coach fares		All households (no.)
	expenditure (£ per week, mean)	households recording expenditure (no.)	expenditure (£ per week, mean)	households recording expenditure (no.)	
Professional & technical	0·63	156	0·41	344	518
Administrative and managerial	0·63	147	0·38	302	472
Teacher	0·28	39	0·31	90	149
Clerical	0·58	146	0·55	325	457
Shop assistant	0·25	13	0·52	41	64
Manual	0·16	402	0·70	2,325	3,011
Selfemployed	0·22	78	0·29	263	492
Retired	0·06	100	0·25	925	1,622
Unemployed	0·21	40	0·51	224	302

Source: Department of Employment.

6.4.4   Special concessions

The much greater than expected response of old people to the GLC's scheme of free off peak travel has already been mentioned. A range of anecdotal evidence suggests that pensioners seem to be making significantly more trips for a variety of different purposes, such as shopping and visiting family, friends and social clubs. Further, although they may sometimes just be enjoying travel for its own sake, the evidence is that they are increasing the number rather than the length of their bus journeys — thus confirming the earlier analysis in this chapter. A similar pattern has also been observed for the response of pensioners to free bus travel in Reading.[7] But the most solid evidence in support of this hypothesis comes from a ten week survey which London Transport undertook at the end of April 1974 as part of a regular investigation into the use made by old people of special travel permits.[8] The survey started a full seven months after the new scheme had been introduced so it should have had time to settle down by then. It was also undertaken at the same time as the previous year's survey, thus improving the reliability of year to year comparisons. Some five hundred of the people with free passes interviewed in the 1974 survey were chosen because they had also participated in the 1973 survey when they held concessionary fare permits. A comparison between the two surveys showed that they had increased their frequency of travel by nearly 30 per cent, accounted for largely by a 40 per cent increase in the Monday–Friday midday off peak period. But the average distance they travelled had barely changed.

Thus a substantial increase in the social welfare of old people seems to have resulted from the GLC's scheme. However, as always with the provision of social services, one group's gain may be another's loss. In particular, there have been complaints about the buses being full of pensioners at the end of the off peak period in the afternoon, which prevents schoolchildren getting home without a long wait. But this is not a criticism of the policy itself. It simply points to the need for careful and flexible management and monitoring of any policy aimed at making special provision for particular social groups.

Children in London have also recently gained another special concession, which gives rise to a potential conflict in another area. This was the GLC's decision, in the March 1975 fares revision, to introduce a 3p bus flat fare for children at all times of day, even in the morning peak when they had previously been charged adult fares. London Transport had advised that it was neither economically desirable nor justifiable that children travelling in the morning rush hour and competing for capacity with adults should pay other than the adult fare; though they recognised that the council might nevertheless wish to introduce such a concession on social grounds. The drawbacks of this change in policy are likely to be particularly acute in the summer holidays, when extra demand from children in peak periods could put further pressure on the already overcrowded buses at a time when the effect of staff shortage on the service is most severe.

During term time the situation is different, as school children have to travel to school and 'compete with adults' for scarce capacity in order to get educated. In Britain it is the local education authorities[9] which have the responsibility for ensuring that children can get to school. Under the Education Act 1944 they are required to provide free transport for or pay the travelling expenses of all children of compulsory school age attending state schools who live over a prescribed distance from the school (two miles for children under eight, and three miles for children of eight or more). Many education authorities also offer concessions for school children not covered by the free travel arrangements. Where the children have to travel by public transport these concessions are usually arranged by asking the public transport operators to issue concessionary travel passes, for which they are reimbursed by the education authorities to make up for the loss in revenue.

In order to remove some of these anomalies, a report of a working party on school transport in England and Wales recommended that there should be a single national flat fare for all school journeys, related to the average cost of a three mile journey. [10] Special exemptions would be made so that free transport would still be available for children from poor families or who suffered from physical or mental handicaps. It was also recommended that the cost of this procedure should be borne by the local education authorities.

On this last point, it would seem right that fares concessions in aid of an identifiable social service should be the responsibility of the authority providing that service. As well as children travelling to school, this principle would also (for example) apply to any special assistance that might be necessary to enable parents to visit their children in hospital or people to visit their relatives in prison.

In Britain the Department of Health and Social Security (DHSS) does have discretion to make payments to those qualifying for supplementary benefits, towards the travelling expenses incurred in making visits to relatives in hospitals, prisons or special schools. In the case of prison visiting, for example, this discretion appears in practice to be exercised on the following lines. After the first three months in prison, the full second class fares paid by a relative for a visit once every four weeks are reimbursed in full by the DHSS to those on low incomes qualifying for supplementary benefit. The fares of the prisoner's children, as well as of his wife, are reimbursed if they are taken on the visit, or alternatively his wife can get a refund for the cost of a help to look after the children while she is away.

These arrangements, however, still place the responsibility for transport on the wrong authority — the DHSS instead of the Home Office. This means, for example, that the Home Office has no incentive to weigh the advantages of having a prisoner near to his family in the initial decision on where to locate him, since the financial penalties of sending him far away are borne by another department. Hence that decision will tend to be dominated almost entirely by other criteria, such as ensuring that high risk prisoners are sent to high security prisons.

A better approach would be to ensure that decisions on special concessions in aid of an identifiable social service are taken by the responsible authority after a careful consideration of the best way of achieving all the objectives of that particular service, taking account of the inevitable conflicts and inconsistencies between them. (These aims would involve specific health, welfare or educational criteria not considered in my list of fares policy objectives.) On the other hand, it is clear that all concessions which have the more general aim of improving travel opportunities for different social groups should be taken by the transport authority in relation to transport criteria. This is especially so as such general concessions may well be available to a substantial proportion of a city's population, and may therefore play a vital role in the local council's transport strategy. In London major general concessions are now available for children up to five (free bus fares) and from 5–15 (low bus flat fare); and for women over 60 and men over 65 (free bus fares). According to the 1971 census of population, these groups between them account for over one third of all people living in London.

In spite of these points, however, the Department of the Environment has decided to exclude all fares concessions for special groups of people as eligible for transport supplementary grant, on the grounds that their purpose is social and not a question of transport policy. This apparent failure to recognise that public transport should also be considered a social service, or at least that social issues should play a vital role in determining decisions on transport policy, is a little disturbing.

6.5 Indirect effects

This section concludes with some brief additional comments about the effects of different fares policies on the location of homes and workplaces, and on the prices of other goods and services.

6.5.1 Effects on location

Any fares policy which changed the comparative costs of journeys of different lengths – such as a change from graduated fares to flat or free fares – could in theory stimulate people into changing where they live or work so as to take full advantage of the new price structure. Thus, for example, a widespread low flat fare or free transport system might encourage people to move to the city's outer suburbs, while still working at the centre as the cost of getting there would no longer be a barrier. However, such effects are unlikely to be anything more than marginal for two reasons. Firstly, as has been shown in this chapter, people are more likely to respond to different fares policies by changing the number rather than the length of their trips. Secondly, even free fares would probably act as only a small ripple on the sea of influences on where people live and work, mainly because of the severe constraints caused by the nature of the housing market, employment opportunities, planning law, social attitudes, and so on. It must be remembered, however, that these constraints have their own dynamic effects. Thus although fares policies may have little effect on location or journey length, the distance people travel may be changing through time for other reasons. In fact the average length of work trips in London (both public and private transport) rose from 3·7 miles in 1962 to 4·3 miles in 1971; which is presumably a reflection of the continuing decentralisation of population and changing structure of employment. [11] Moreover, although car ownership does not seem to have much influence on the length of public transport journeys at any one point in time, the rise in car ownership may have encouraged certain land use changes which tend to increase journey lengths through time − the substitution of supermarkets for small neighbourhood shops, for example.

6.5.2 *Effects on other prices*

A low fares policy financed by higher taxation (whether through rates or otherwise) would spread its effects to the prices of goods and services throughout the city and beyond its boundaries. The magnitude and direction of these effects should ideally be explored by looking at a number of different factors. First, there is the question touched on briefly in the second section, of how firms would pass on their higher taxes in higher prices. Using the classical assumptions of microeconomic theory, Appendix 6A.3 shows that in a perfectly competitive market, prices would rise by a proportion which is approximately equal to

$$\frac{\eta_s}{\eta_s - \eta_d} \times t$$

where η_s, η_d, are the point elasticities of supply and demand for the goods in question with respect to their price, and t is the extra tax charge as a percentage of the firm's turnover. However, in London, as in most conurbations, there are numerous cartels and government pressures towards price control which make the market anything but perfectly competitive, and highlight the difficulties of producing reliable estimates.

Then there is what economists call people's 'marginal propensity to consume', rather than save, in response to increases in real income. It is, of course, much higher for poorer than for richer people, and hence a key parameter in studies of income distribution.

Finally, it is necessary to investigate the trading relationships of firms with other firms and consumers in the city, in the rest of the country and overseas. Such an investigation, which would probably have to be carried out using a regional input−output model, would lead to estimates of the extent to which prices rise within as opposed to beyond the city's boundaries.

Any attempt to unravel these complications would go far beyond the scope of this book. They do, however, expose the weakness of the simple parameter a used in Appendix 6A.1, and emphasise the need for further research in this area.

APPENDICES

6A.1 The effects on income distribution of changes in fare and rate levels

In order to work out the effects of paying for the increased costs of public transport in a British city through fares or rates, assume that there are N_i households in the ith income group into which the city's households have been divided, whose mean expenditures on rates and public transport fares are R_i, F_i respectively. The R_i are assumed to include an allowance for those who are not owner occupiers and who effectively pay rates through the rent — the Family Expenditure Survey makes a similar assumption. Then for all households

$$\text{total rates paid} = \Sigma R_i N_i = RN$$
$$\begin{array}{l}\text{total expenditure}\\\text{on public transport}\end{array} = \Sigma F_i N_i = FN$$

where $N = \Sigma N_i$ and R, F, are the mean expenditures for the city as a whole.

For simplicity the argument is developed for London though the method can be generally applied. Assume that public transport costs rise by ΔC, and contrast two extreme methods of meeting them — entirely from the rates, or entirely from fares.[12]

In the former case the extra expenditure of the ith group of households will be

$$(0.4\, p_i + 0.6a) \frac{R_i N_i}{RN}\, \Delta C \qquad (6A.1)$$

where p_i is the proportion paid in rates net of rebates, and it is assumed that a constant proportion a of the increased rates paid by nondomestic concerns is passed on in higher prices of goods and services bought by Londoners. (In London some 40 per cent of total rates paid comes from households, and 60 per cent from commercial, industrial and other undertakings).

Under the high fare policy, if all income groups reacted in a similar manner to the higher fares (i.e. if their price elasticities of demand were identical), then the extra expenditure of the ith group of households would be

$$\frac{F_i N_i}{FN}(1 - \beta) \, \Delta C \tag{6A.2}$$

where β is the proportion of fares income derived from non-London residents (principally tourists and commuters across the GLC boundary).

In practice, however, the poorer households are likely to have higher demand elasticities. The evidence discussed in the main text implies that they would react to higher fares by making proportionately fewer trips, though they would tend to travel just as far on each trip. By this process the richer households would in fact be bearing a higher proportion of the increased costs than is indicated in (6A.2) above. There is also the point that travellers tend to respond to price changes according to the nature of the service provided: underground passengers, in particular, tend to have lower demand elasticities than bus passengers. However, since people with lower demand elasticities (whether because they are richer, or using a higher quality service, or both) would also be buying comparatively more trips for their money, (6A.2) would seem to be the best neutral assumption to make in calculating the effects on income distribution of the high fare policy.

The net gain of a high rate over a high fare policy ((6A.2)–(6A.1)) for the ith group of households is thus

$$\frac{N_i}{N} \left\{ \frac{F_i}{F} (1-\beta) - \frac{R_i}{R} (0.4 \, p_i + 0.6a) \right\} \Delta C \tag{6A.3}$$

which will be positive if, and only if,

$$RF_i (1-\beta) > R_i F (0.4 \, p_i + 0.6a) \tag{6A.4}$$

We have not yet considered what kind of fares changes are involved in the expression F_i/F. The data in Table 6A.1 show that the richest households would 'lose' more than four times as much as the poorest households from higher underground fares alone, ($F_3/F = 1.7$, $F_1/F = 0.4$ for underground fares); but from higher bus fares they lose less than twice as much ($F_3/F = 1.1$, $F_1/F = 0.7$ for bus fares).

This suggests that a low fares policy would be considerably more progressive if it applied more to bus than to underground fares. However, since differential fares policies of this kind could cause operational problems concerned with the excessive diversion from the railways that

130

Table 6A.1

Household expenditure on fares and rates: by gross household income (Greater London, 1971−72)

| | Gross household income (£ per week, mean) | | | |
	0−30	30−60	60+	All
Household expenditure on:				
bus	0·28	0·44	0·47	0·41
underground	0·18	0·43	0·83	0·49
bus and underground	0·46	0·87	1·30	0·90
rates:				
before rebates	1·19	1·43	1·80	1·48
after rebates	1·11	1·43*	1·79*	1·46

Sources: GLTS 1971−72 (bus and underground fares), FES 1972 (rates).
*These numbers reflect a very small amount of rate rebate − 0·4p for the £30−60 income group, and 0·5p for the £60+ income group.

might take place if bus fares were too low in relation to underground fares, the simplest operational policy would be one which applied equally to bus and underground fares. On that basis, and using the figures in Table 6A.1, relation (6A.4) above shows that the net gain of the high rate over the high fare policy will be positive for the three groups of households if, and only if,

for households earning £0−30 per week

$$0·6p_1 + 0·9a + \beta < 1 \qquad (6A.5)$$

for households earning £30−60 per week

$$0·4p_2 + 0·6a + \beta < 1 \qquad (6A.6)$$

for households earning more than £60 per week

$$0·3p_3 + 0·5a + \beta < 1 \qquad (6A.7)$$

These relations indicate that provided

1 the poorest households get decent rate rebates (i.e. p_1 is sufficiently low); and
2 not too great a proportion of the extra rate charges incurred by firms

131

are passed on in higher prices paid by Londoners (i.e. a is sufficiently low); and

3 revenue from nonLondon residents does not account for too high a proportion of total fares revenue (i.e. β is sufficiently low);

then all households will gain absolutely from a high rate policy.

Considering these three points in turn, Table 6A.1 shows that in 1972 the two higher income groups received an insignificant amount of rate rebate (i.e. p_2 and p_3 were approximately equal to one) and that the average rebate for the £0–30 group was some 7 per cent (i.e. $p_1 = 0.93$). However, the scheme has become considerably more generous since then. Because of their complexities the current impact of rate rebates could only be calculated precisely if sufficient information were available about typical family structures in relation to average household incomes: information which is not available at present. However, an intuitive guess based on the kinds of rebates that can now be obtained suggests that p_1 might be down to as low as 0.50.

Similarly the impact of the higher rate charges borne by nondomestic concerns can only be guessed. Some of them would be absorbed, and some passed on in higher prices of goods and services bought by nonLondon residents. An intuitive judgement based on the structure of the nondomestic undertakings who pay rates in London[13] suggests that a maximum upper limit for a would be 0.50.

The third parameter, β, can fortunately be calculated more precisely. GLTS data imply that it is about 0.15 for bus and underground in total (i.e. some 15 per cent of London Transport's fares revenue comes from nonLondoners). If bus and underground are considered separately, however, the figures are 10 per cent and 20 per cent respectively. The lower figure for buses implies once again that a low fares policy is more progressive if adopted for buses alone, provided, of course, it is operationally feasible to introduce such a policy.

Using those estimates for the three key parameters (p, a, β) it can be seen from relations (6A.5)–(6A.7) that all three groups of households gain absolutely from a high rate policy. In terms of the earlier definition (p. 106) the high rate policy will be progressive if the gain for the poorest households is greater when expressed as a proportion of disposable household income (it is smaller in absolute terms). It can be derived from expression (6A.3) that the high rate policy will be progressive as between the poorest and richest households if, and only if,

$$\frac{N_3 Y_1}{N_1 Y_3} \left\{ \frac{F_3}{F} (1-\beta) - \frac{R_3}{R} (0.4 + 0.6a) \right\} < \frac{F_1}{F} (1-\beta) - \frac{R_1}{R} (0.4p + 0.6a)$$

where y refers to disposable income, and it is assumed that $p_3 = 1$, $p_1 = p$.

132

Using once again the Table 6A.1 data (and assuming that N_1, N_2, N_3 are in the same proportion as in the FES sample, namely 235:338:277) the following inequality can be derived

$$1 \cdot 3p + 1 \cdot 1a + 0 \cdot 5\beta < 1 \qquad (6A.8)$$

It can similarly be shown that the high rate policy will be progressive as between low and medium, and medium and high, income households respectively if and only if the following relations hold (assuming $p_2 = p_3 = 1$, $p_1 = p < 1$):

$$2 \cdot 1p + 0 \cdot 8a - 0 \cdot 6\beta < 1 \qquad (6A.9)$$

$$1 \cdot 6a + 2 \cdot 1\beta \qquad < 1 \qquad (6A.10)$$

If we assume as before that $p = a = 0 \cdot 5$, $\beta = 0 \cdot 15$, then these inequalities imply that a low fares policy (applied in precisely the same way to both bus and underground fares, and with no assistance from central government except via the rate rebates) is regressive. However, the left hand sides of these relations are only just greater than one so it would not take much to tip the balance. In particular, if it were possible to restrict a low fares policy just to the buses, this would be progressive even if financed entirely from the rates. For the relations corresponding to (6A.8)–(6A.10) as a test of whether such a policy change would be progressive (which can again be derived from Table 6A.1, this time using just the bus and rate expenditure figures) are as shown below. And all three of them easily hold with $p = a = 0 \cdot 5$, and with β for buses now down to $0 \cdot 10$ (instead of $0 \cdot 15$ as previously). Indeed, it can be shown that the bottom gains slightly more than the top income group even when the gains are expressed in absolute terms, rather than as proportions of disposable income.

$$0 \cdot 6p + 0 \cdot 6a + 0 \cdot 7\beta < 1 \qquad (6A.8)^*$$

$$1 \cdot 2p + 0 \cdot 5a + 0 \cdot 1\beta < 1 \qquad (6A.9)^*$$

$$0 \cdot 7a + 1 \cdot 4\beta < 1 \qquad (6A.10)^*$$

6A.2 The relationship between household trip making and household income

This appendix investigates — for London households — the statistical relationships between their mean fare per public transport trip (L) (the proxy for trip length), the number of trips taken per day (T),[14] and the mean fares expenditure per day (F), all with respect to the household's gross income (Y).

The first three variables are related by the identity

$$F = LT$$

As a start, it is sensible to hypothesise a simple relationship of the form

$$F = f(Y)$$

If $\eta(L)$, $\eta(T)$ and $\eta(F)$ denote the point elasticities of the variables in brackets with respect to Y, then

$$\eta(F) = \frac{dF}{dY} \cdot \frac{Y}{F}$$

$$= \frac{d}{dY}(LT) \cdot \frac{Y}{LT}$$

$$= \frac{dL}{dY} \cdot \frac{Y}{L} + \frac{dT}{dY} \cdot \frac{Y}{T}$$

$$\eta(F) = \eta(L) + \eta(T)$$

This shows that the overall response of household fares expenditure to changes in household income at any income level, can be estimated by simply adding the elasticities of fares per trip and number of trips at the same income level. Thus we only need estimate the relationships

$$L = g(Y)$$
$$T = h(Y)$$

and derive the necessary information for F without setting up a new model.

Unlike the case with the price elasticities discussed in Chapter 4, these income elasticities are likely to be positive for the majority of households: in other words, most households are likely to respond to increases in income by travelling more often or over longer distances. According to the form of the relationship, however, there may eventually come a point at which this response works in the opposite direction. This would arise if the elasticities declined in such a way that they became negative above a certain income level.

6A.2.1 *Bus Trips*

For the reasons explained in the annex to this appendix, the best form of relationship between bus trip rate and income is likely to be

$$\log T = -a + b\log Y - c(\log Y)^2$$

(with a, b, c all positive).

And in fact that form of relationship gives a very close fit to the data, namely

$$\log T = -19 \cdot 48 + 5 \cdot 04 \log Y - 0 \cdot 32 (\log Y)^2$$
$$(0 \cdot 43) \qquad (0 \cdot 03)$$
$$\text{(6A.11)}$$

The multiple correlation coefficient is remarkably high ($\overline{R}^2 = 0 \cdot 96$) [15] and the standard errors (shown in brackets) indicate that both coefficients are statistically significant at the 1 per cent confidence level.

However, this high correlation is a little spurious, since it is partly accounted for by the fact that two other variables embodied in the income terms cause income and trip rate to be closely related to each other. These variables are household size and the level of car ownership, both of which increase with income as well as having a strong influence on trip rate. To distil a cleaner relationship between trip making and household income, the effect of household size and car ownership must be separated out. The obvious statistical technique for this purpose is the dummy variable, which was used to derive the following equation:

$$\log T = -14 \cdot 39 + 3 \cdot 71 \log Y - 0 \cdot 24(\log Y)^2 - 0 \cdot 76 C_1 - 1 \cdot 10 C_2$$
$$(1 \cdot 07) \qquad (0 \cdot 07) \qquad (0 \cdot 09) \qquad (0 \cdot 09)$$
$$\text{(6A.12)}$$
$$+ 0 \cdot 62 H_2 + 1 \cdot 01 H_3 + 1 \cdot 33 H_4 + 1 \cdot 59 H_5$$
$$(0 \cdot 11) \quad (0 \cdot 11) \quad (0 \cdot 11) \quad (0 \cdot 11)$$

where $C_1 = 1$ for households which own one car, 0 otherwise
$C_2 = 1$ for households which own two or more cars, 0 otherwise; and the other dummy variables are defined in a similar manner so that H_2, H_3, H_4, H_5 are 1 for households with 2, 3, 4, and 5 or more persons respectively, and zero otherwise. The base equation with just the constant and income terms is thus the estimator of the numbers of trips made by one person households without cars.

Once again the correlation coefficient ($\overline{R}^2 = 0 \cdot 64$) is exceptionally high, especially as the number of observations has grown from 10 to 150 as a result of including the dummy variables; and all coefficients are still significant at the 1 per cent level. Further, as well as matching the empirical evidence very closely, this equation has the convenient property that the elasticity of trip making with respect to household income turns out to depend just on the level of income, and not on how many people the household contains or on whether a car is owned.

As for the relationship between trip length and income, the problem of decline at higher income levels does not arise. Nor does household size appear to have much influence. And although there is a significant effect

135

arising from car ownership (which will be considered later), it is appropriate and convenient to keep to a simple relationship (without the use of dummy variables) in order to study the influence of income on trip length for the 'average' household.

The annex explains why the most appropriate relationship between L and Y is given by the equation

$$\log L = 1 \cdot 70 - 117 \cdot 01 \quad \frac{1}{Y + 51 \cdot 48} \qquad (6A.13)$$
$$(13 \cdot 65)$$

This equation again has all the right properties, including a very high correlation between observed and estimated values of L ($R^2 = 0 \cdot 90$) and a highly significant (at the 1 per cent confidence level) coefficient of the independent variable.

6A.2.2 Rail Trips

For the relationship between rail trip rate and household income, an equation can be found which not only fits the data very closely, but also has the intuitively plausible property that income elasticity declines as income grows. This equation is

$$\log T = 0 \cdot 44 - 1156 \cdot 38 \cdot \frac{1}{Y} \qquad (6A.14)$$
$$(95 \cdot 40)$$

Although the correlation coefficient is not as good as with the corresponding bus equation (6A.11), it is still extremely high ($R^2 = 0 \cdot 94$). And the coefficient of $\frac{1}{Y}$ is significant at the 1 per cent level. Once again, however, the correlation is a little spurious as we have not yet accounted for household size and car ownership. The disaggregated equation corresponding to (6A.12), which takes these influences into account, is

$$\log T = -0 \cdot 18 - 485 \cdot 46 \cdot \frac{1}{Y} -0 \cdot 49C_1 -0 \cdot 70C_2$$
$$(86 \cdot 75) \quad (0 \cdot 14) \quad (0 \cdot 14)$$
$$+0 \cdot 17H_2 + 0 \cdot 80H_3 + 0 \cdot 77H_4 + 0 \cdot 84H_5 \qquad (6A.15)$$
$$(0 \cdot 19) \quad (0 \cdot 19) \quad (0 \cdot 19) \quad (0 \cdot 19)$$

with the dummy variables defined in precisely the same way as before.

This time the correlation is much lower than with (6A.12) but still highly significant and perfectly respectable for a cross sectional analysis with 150 observations ($R^2 = 0 \cdot 27$). [16] All coefficients are significant at the 1 per cent confidence level, except for H_2 where the standard error is greater than the coefficient. It should also be noted that the coefficients

136

of H_3, H_4 and H_5 are of the same order of magnitude. In fact the differences between these coefficients are not statistically significant, though each coefficient on its own is highly significant. This means that although household size has a significant influence on trip rate, it is reflected only in the difference between 1 and 2 person households on the one hand, and 3 or more person households on the other. With buses, by contrast, household size not only has a bigger impact on trip rate (the coefficient of H_5 in (6A.12) is nearly twice the size of the corresponding coefficient in (6A.15)), but trip rates increase in a regular and statistically significant pattern through each household size.

It could be that increasing household size has less influence on rail travel because housewives and children travel much less by train than by bus. But more detailed analysis would be needed to test an hypothesis of that kind. Meanwhile, equation (6A.15) takes sufficient account of the influence of household size to enable us to be confident in using it to take account of the direct relationship between trip rate and household income.

For the relationship between the rail trip lengths of ordinary single ticket holders and their household income, the most appropriate equation is

$$\log L = 3 \cdot 49 + 2838 \cdot 53 \quad \frac{1}{Y + 2193} \qquad (6A.16)$$
$$(403 \cdot 03)$$

for which $\overline{R}^2 = 0 \cdot 88$, and the Y coefficient is significant at the 1 per cent level.

6A.2.3   Car ownership

The effect of car ownership on bus and rail trip rates was taken into account by including dummy variables for car ownership in equations (6A.12) and (6A.15). The fact that the independent variable in those equations is $\log T$ rather than T means that car ownership has the effect of changing T by the same proportion at all income levels. More specifically, car ownership causes a substantial proportionate reduction in the number of trips made on both buses and trains, in view of the fact that the coefficients of the dummy variables are negative and fairly high in both equations. With fare per trip (but not trip rate) no statistically significant influence of car ownership could be detected as far as railways were concerned. With the buses, however, highly significant results were obtained. The best ordinary least squares fit to the data came from an equation which changed the slope as well as the position of the previous curve (6A.13) by putting a dummy variable for car ownership with the income term. The result is given in equation (6A.17).

$$\log L = 1\cdot66 - 96\cdot43 \cdot \frac{1}{Y+51\cdot48} + 42\cdot17 \cdot \frac{C}{Y+51\cdot48} \quad (6A.17)$$
$$(16\cdot32) \qquad\qquad (16\cdot54)$$
$$(\bar{R}^2 = 0\cdot61)$$

where $C = 1$ for households with one or more cars, 0 otherwise.

This equation shows that the average fare paid on the buses still rises with income for households without cars, but barely changes at all for households with cars. For example, it can be calculated that at a low income of £400 a year the average fare paid per bus trip of passengers from households without cars was 4·2p. The effect of owning one or more cars was to increase the average to 4·7p i.e. by over 10 per cent. But at the median household income of £1,750 a year, the gap had narrowed to only 2 per cent (the averages being 5·1p and 5·0p for households with and without cars respectively). However, the fact that the coefficient of car/income term is both positive and statistically significant (at the 2 per cent confidence level) suggests that people who live in car owning households do make slightly longer bus journeys on average at all income levels, even though the difference is very small indeed at high incomes. Car ownership also has the effect of reducing the coefficient of the income term by nearly half (from 96·43 to 54·26). This implies that the elasticities of car owning households are approximately that much lower at all income levels. However, by the same token the elasticities of households without cars are significantly higher than the 'average' figures given in Table 6.2.

6A.2.4   *Annex*

Bus trips: relation between trip rate (T), fare per trip (L) and household income (Y)

This appendix considers in turn how to specify the most suitable relationship between T and Y for buses, and between L and Y for railways as well. It should be noted that the form of these relationships has a strong influence on the values of the point elasticities upon which much of the analysis rests. It is quite possible for two curves to be barely distinguishable on statistical 'goodness of fit' tests, yet to yield widely different elasticities at extreme values of the independent variable. This means that in choosing the form of relationship, it is essential for the standard statistical tests to be supported by separate hypotheses about the shape of the curve, particularly at either end of the range.

138

(i) *Relation between* **T** *and* **Y**

The relationship between T and Y must take account of the fact that for buses, the trip rate first rises to a peak and then falls off at higher incomes. This means that some kind of quadratic relationship must be sought.

Although the straightforward quadratic

$$T = a + bY - cY^2 \qquad (6A.18)$$

(with a, b, c all positive)

gives a good ordinary least squares fit to the data, it has the drawback that the estimated equation fails to pass through the origin, so that the trip rate is not zero at zero income, which is contrary to common sense.

Another possibility, which gets nearer to what we want, is

$$\log T = -a + b\log Y - cY^2 \qquad (6A.19)$$

For here the curve at least goes towards the origin (T tends to zero as Y tends to zero). However, the elasticity is given by

$$\eta = b - 2cY^2$$

$$\text{Hence } \frac{d\eta}{dY} = -4cY, \quad \text{and}$$

$$\frac{d^2\eta}{dY^2} = -4c$$

Since both these derivatives are negative for $Y > 0$, the elasticity not only decreases as Y increases (which is plausible), but the rate of decrease is accelerating (which is not).

This leads us to look for a third possibility –

$$\log T = -a + b\log Y - c(\log Y)^2 \qquad (6A.20)$$

This curve also approaches the origin (i.e. T tends to zero with Y). Further, the elasticity is given by

$$\eta = b - 2c\log Y$$

with

$$\frac{d\eta}{dY} = -\frac{2c}{Y}$$

This means that η is once again decreasing for all $Y > 0$ (since $\dfrac{d\eta}{dY}$ is negative). This time, however, its rate of decrease is slowing down (since $\dfrac{d^2\eta}{dY^2}$ is positive), which is a much more plausible result. Equation (6A.20) also gives a closer fit to the data than equation (6A.19) (i.e. it has a higher R^2), as well as being a neater and more consistent equation from the analytical point of view. The only possible drawback is that there is a high multicollinearity between $\log Y$ and $(\log Y)^2$, which is greater than that between $\log Y$ and Y^2. However, since we are only interested in the relationship between T and Y, and not in the separate influence on T of either $\log Y$ or $(\log Y)^2$, this statistical problem is of no relevance to the analysis and does not detract from the superiority of (6A.20) over (6A.19). For these reasons equation (6A.20) was chosen as the basis for specifying the relationship between T and Y. The only slight oddity to be noted (which applies to equation (6A.19) as well as (6A.20)) is that there is a point of inflexion near to the origin. That is, the slope of the curve, $\frac{dT}{dY}$, increases until it reaches the inflexion point, and then decreases for all higher values of Y. It can be calculated that this point is given by

$$\log Y = \frac{2b - \sqrt{1+8c} - 1}{4c}$$

Applying that formula to equation (6A.12), this means that the point of inflexion is reached at an income of £135 per annum, which is low enough to give confidence that this phenomenon will not significantly distort the results obtained.

(ii) *Relation between* **L** *and* **Y**
With this relation the problem of finding a suitable quadratic equation does not arise. But there is instead an equally awkward difficulty arising from the fact that the curve should not this time be expected to pass through the origin. For common sense tells us that the fare per trip, as a proxy for trip length, should tend to a positive value as income tends to zero. Moreover, the fare per trip should also have a positive, but finite, value at the other end of the range (when income tends to infinity).

At first sight the two equations

$$L = a - \frac{b}{Y}, \quad \text{and}$$

$$\log L = a - \frac{b}{Y}$$

seem to be suitable candidates. For they both have finite solutions for infinite values of Y, as well as giving good fits to the data. But they both have to be rejected as they fail to have the right properties at the origin. In

140

fact with the first curve the fare per trip not only becomes negative but actually tends to minus infinity as income tends to zero (it is a rectangular hyperbola with the L axis as an asymptote): which means that it is pulled down further than it should be at lower income levels, thus suggesting higher elasticities at lower incomes than is justified by reasonable hypotheses. Further, although the second equation is better as it at least touches the Y axis at the origin (L has a minimum value there), that advantage is offset by the fact that it has an inflexion near the origin (at $Y = \frac{1}{2}b$): which again has the effect of pulling the curve down too much at the lower income levels.

The obvious way of tackling this problem is to see what happens if the curves are shifted to the left by a distance c, say, thus in effect replacing Y in the above equations by $Y+c$. The curves might then cut the L axis at a positive value of L, as required. Thus for example the new rectangular hyperbola will be of the form

$$L = a - \frac{b}{Y+c}$$

whose asymptotes are $L = a$ and $Y = -c$, and which cuts the L axis at $L = a - \dfrac{b}{c}$

Such an equation could only be fitted directly by ordinary least squares if the value of c was known in advance — which is, of course, not the case. That difficulty was surmounted in the following way. First, preliminary values of a, b and c were guessed from broad judgements about the likely position of the curve and of the asymptotes. These values were then fed into a computer to be moulded by an iterative program (BMD X85) which has the effect of minimising the error sum of squares. The regression equation was then re-estimated by ordinary least squares, using the value of c obtained from the iterative procedure.

With the rectangular hyperbola, the best fit obtained by that process for bus fare per trip was

$$L = 5 \cdot 45 - \underset{(70 \cdot 87)}{628 \cdot 57} \cdot \frac{1}{Y + 104 \cdot 20}$$

Although this equation is an improvement on the previous version, L is still negative ($- 0 \cdot 6$) when Y is zero. This is because the mathematics of a rectangular hyperbola are such that it does not get pulled down quickly enough as income rises, so that the vertical asymptote can only be shifted far enough over to the left to make the curve cut the L axis above the origin, at the expense of getting a worse fit at the higher income levels.

The logarithmic equation, however, does not run into those difficulties, and the best fit for bus fare per trip obtained from the iterative procedure was that shown as equation (6A.13). It cuts the L axis at a positive value ($L = +0.6$ when $Y = 0$), and touches the Y axis at its minimum value when $Y = -51.5$. The point of inflexion occurs at $Y = 7.0$, which is so close to zero income that any distortions this might cause will be insignificant. Equation (6A.17) was then obtained by ordinary least squares, keeping the value of c found for equation (6A.13), namely 51.48.

The rail fare per trip equation (6A.16) was obtained in a corresponding manner. It cuts the L axis at $L = +9.0$, touches the Y axis at $Y = -2193$, and has its point of inflexion at $Y = -774$.

A final point to be noted about both the bus and rail fare per trip equations is that the elasticities increase at first and only decline after they have reached a maximum value, which occurs at $Y = c$. With the bus equation (6A.13) the maximum elasticity is thus at $Y = 51.5$, which is so low that it can be said that the bus fare per trip elasticity declines through virtually the whole income range. With the rail equation (6A.16), however, the maximum elasticity occurs at $Y = 2183$, which is above the median income of 1750. Hence the rail fare per trip elasticity increases through over half the full income range, and only begins to decline at higher income levels.

6A.3 Effect of tax increases on firms' prices

Using the classical assumptions of microeconomic theory, Figure 6A.1 on facing page shows a firm's supply and demand curves intersecting at the equilibrium point (P_1, Q_1). Now assume that the extra tax that is imposed (whether through a rates increase or otherwise) represents a proportion t of the firm's turnover. Then the supply curve S_1 is shifted vertically upwards by a distance $t\,PQ/Q = tP$ (for all P), making the new supply curve S_2 which intersects the same demand curve D at the new equilibrium position (P_2, Q_2).

If we assume that the demand curve D and supply curve S_1 have constant point elasticities η_d (<0) and η_s (>0) between (P_1, Q_1) and (P_2, Q_2), their equations along that range are

$$\log Q = a + \eta_d \log P \qquad (D)$$

$$\log Q = b + \eta_s \log P \qquad (S_1)$$

Fig. 6A.1　Supply and demand curves after tax increase

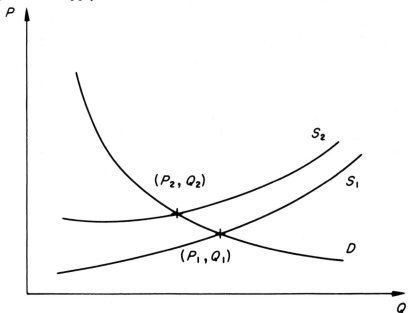

The equation of S_2 can then be derived as

$$\log Q = b + \eta_s \log \frac{1}{1+t} P \quad (S_2)$$

Now since the points P_1 and P_2 are given by the intersection of D and S_1, and D and S_2, respectively, solving those equations simultaneously in turn gives

$$(\eta_s - \eta_d) \log P_1 = a - b$$

$$\eta_s \log \frac{1}{1+t_2} P_2 - \eta_d \log P_2 = a - b$$

(where t_2 is the value of t at (P_2, Q_2))

Hence

$$(\eta_s - \eta_d) \log P_1 = (\eta_s - \eta_d) \log P_2 - \eta_s \log (1+t_2)$$

or

$$\log P_2 - \log P_1 = \frac{\eta_s}{\eta_s - \eta_d} \log(1+t_2)$$

If p is the proportional price increase following the tax change,

$$P_2 = (1+p)P_1$$

therefore

$$\log(1+p) = \frac{\eta_s}{\eta_s - \eta_d} \log(1+t_2) \tag{6A.21}$$

We are not quite there yet as what we really need to have is a relationship between p and t_1, the value of t at the starting position (P_1, Q_1). The two values $(t_1$ and $t_2)$ will, of course, be the same if t is constant, as with a sales tax, for example: in which case the above formula can be used directly to calculate p from the known value of t_1. Other situations, however, may be more complicated. Thus if the total tax levy (rather than the proportion) is the same at the new and old positions, then

$$t_2 P_2 Q_2 = t_1 P_1 Q_1$$

which gives

$$(1+p)^{\eta_d+1} t_2 = t_1$$

hence substituting in (6A.21) will give a complicated polynomial relationship between p and t_1 which could be difficult to solve.

For small changes, however t_2 and t_1 will be virtually indistinguishable. Moreover, in these circumstances we can approximate to the first order (i.e. expand by power series ignoring squared terms and higher) − which leads to the simple formula

$$p = \frac{\eta_s}{\eta_s - \eta_d} \times t_1$$

Notes

[1] The information is derived mainly from *Family Expenditure Survey Report for 1972*, HMSO, 1973, and supplementary data supplied by the Department of Employment. Although FES data for later years are now available, the 1972 report has been the main source since it covers a similar time period to the GLTS survey.

[2] For a general summary of the main results of this survey, see *Greater London Transportation Survey: Initial Results*, GLC Research Report No. 18, 1974.

[3] See, for example, D.A. Nevitt, 'The Burden of Domestic Rates', *Policy and Politics*, September 1973.

[4] Greater London Council Budget 1975−76 and Projections 1976−80.

[5] See Chapter 4, Appendix 4A.1, for a rigorous definition of point elasticity and other elasticity concepts.

[6] This reinforces the findings of M. Hillman as reported in *Travel Needs of Individuals,* Transport and Road Research Laboratory Supplementary Report 37UC, 1974.

[7] A.J. Daly, 'Pensioners' Jaunts', *New Society,* 29 August 1974.

[8] J.D. Freeman, *Free Travel for the Elderly in London — 1974 Survey,* London Transport Operational Research Report R208, 1975.

[9] In the metropolitan conurbations and in Greater London these are different to the authorities responsible for public transport: they are the district (rather than the county) councils in the former case, and the Inner London Education Authority together with the outer borough councils (rather than the Greater London Council) in the latter.

[10] *School Transport,* HMSO, 1973.

[11] See *Greater London Transportation Survey: Initial Results,* op.cit.

[12] There is no loss of generality in presenting the argument in this way. The conclusions stand for any change in financing as between fares and rates.

[13] See *Annual Abstract of Greater London Statistics 1972,* Table 12.03.

[14] A trip has been defined in the analysis as a complete public transport journey for which a separate fare is paid. In technical jargon, this is a *stage* as far as bus trips are concerned, and a *semi-linked journey* for rail trips.

[15] $\bar{R}$ denotes the multiple correlation coefficient corrected for degrees of freedom. This statistic (here and elsewhere) has also been calculated as the correlation between the observed and estimated values of T, not of the dependent variable $\log T$. Both these corrections result in lower values of $\bar{R}^2$, except in Equations (6A.13) and (6A.16) where the latter correction leads to a very slight increase.

[16] The F ratio is 13·37, which confirms that the regression is highly significant. Even a value as low as 2·8 would have been sufficient to ensure significance at the 1 per cent level.

7   Conclusions

Although the practice of charging fares to public transport passengers which reflect the full cost of the services they use is under strong attack for being an antisocial, environmentally disruptive, and indeed inefficient way of tackling urban transport problems, the numerous defenders of it have a good case to argue, and find it relatively easy to defend their position since there is as yet no consensus about a better alternative for this important area of public policy. These disagreements have involved heated public discussion in many countries between leaders of opinion such as elected politicians (of all complexions), journalists, employers' organisations, trades unions, and voluntary pressure groups of one kind and another. And such conflicting pressures are now pushing public transport towards a critical turning point in its history, similar to that which other public services passed through in earlier periods.

7.1   Social service policies

As far as charging for education is concerned, for example, many European countries followed a similar pattern of development during the nineteenth century, with the state gradually becoming involved in heavier subsidisation of the service (and taking over from the churches the chief responsibility for its provision) leading to the point at which it became available at no charge for all children between certain ages. In England the first government grant to the church schools was made in 1833, in return for which powers were taken to inspect them. The sum was £20,000 compared with £50,000 spent on the royal stables during the year. The grants increased to reach over £800,000 in 1861; though as an interesting parallel with certain current views towards the provision of public transport, they dropped back over the next few years as a result of the introduction of a system of 'payment by results' according to attendance and success in passing exams. But this was only a temporary setback, and the practice was phased out by the end of the century. In 1870 the state became directly involved in educational provision by setting up schools run by locally elected school boards. By 1918 school fees were finally abolished in all the elementary schools controlled or assisted by the state.

Another interesting illustration is provided by the setting up of the free National Health Service in the United Kingdom in 1946. Before then, there had been a bewildering variety of provisions and entitlements in which local authorities, diverse voluntary bodies and insurance agencies all played a part. Under the National Insurance Act of 1911, for example, manual workers and nonmanual employees earning less than £160 a year (a limit which was raised to £250 in 1919 and £420 in 1942) were enabled to obtain certain free medical services, including general practitioner services operated by local insurance committees under what was known as the 'panel' system. But a comprehensive medical service was only available to those who could afford to pay for it, as the fortitude and knowledge required to obtain access to particular services and break through the various 'means testing' barriers was beyond the scope of the less well off. The particular form of comprehensive national health service proposed after the second world war nevertheless gave rise to sharp conflict, with the main disputes leading up to the 1946 Act taking place between the government, through the Minister of Health Aneurin Bevan, and the medical profession.

Many of the arguments that came up in the conflicts between church and state over education, and between the government and the doctors over health, were similar to those now being used in the public transport debate; and covered a whole series of disagreements about quality, standards and ethics, and the roles of various types of organisation in meeting them. Thus it was argued, for instance, that it was a misuse of public funds to make the health service free for everybody, including those who could afford to pay for it. But there are many points that can and have been made to counter such a proposition, some of which are similar to those that have been touched on in earlier chapters. And many British protagonists of free urban public transport would now maintain that it is right for the state to ensure that this important public service is made available to everybody at little or no charge, in the same way that education, libraries, hospitals and other public services are provided. It is claimed that this is the best way of making sure that the less privileged members of society have the opportunity to travel in order to visit family and friends, to engage in various kinds of leisure activity, or to have access to as wide a range of jobs as those who are better off: all of which are needed for getting the most out of life. And it makes no more sense to charge the market price for travel on buses and trains than for learning how to read and write, borrowing a book from the library or going to hospital.

7.2　Pricing philosophies

This has been described in Chapter 3 as the welfare state approach to public expenditure, and contrasted with the nationalised industry approach under which the consumer pays the full cost of the service provided, apart from any special assistance that may be offered to identified people in need. Successive British governments actually departed from the latter approach in the early 1970s, when all nationalised industry prices were restrained to grow at a much slower rate than costs, leading to mounting deficits which had to be met by central government grant: that is out of the taxpayer's instead of the consumer's pocket. But in early 1975 the government went back to the previous policy of trying to make the industries cover their costs in full out of income from consumers. This resulted in large price increases, which were particularly sharp for the electricity and postal services. The worsening economic position in 1975 also led the government to put strong pressure on local authorities and public transport operators to put in the largest fares increases they could manage, thus giving a further twist to the 'commercial viability' approach to public transport announced the previous year. But the approach was far from consistent, perhaps the biggest irony being the government's decision in April 1975 to inject enormous public subsidies into the motor car industry (some £700 million of loan and equity capital between 1975 and 1978) as part of the rescue operation for British Leyland.

The contrast between these approaches is also reflected in broader political theories about the prices to be charged for public services. These range from the purest forms of communism, under which the state is responsible not only for the production of all goods and services, but also for their distribution according to some kind of rationing device, with no prices being charged for any of them; to pure capitalism under which the production and distribution of public services as well as consumer goods takes place in a freely competitive market, with prices (and incomes) determined automatically by the interaction of supply and demand in the market place, with minimal state intervention, and with help for the poor and needy largely dependent on voluntary initiative and enterprise. In practice, however, these essentially nineteenth century extremes are not appropriate for the management of any modern economy. All countries tend to be run so that prices are charged for some services and not for others; and there are no hard and fast rules which can be used to determine whether the boundary line has been drawn in the right place in any one country — whether, for example, the British are right to have free education and health, but full price gas and electricity. With public transport the lack of dependence of the actual practice in pricing policy on traditional political theories can be seen from the fact that a range of different policies towards fare levels are followed, for example, by administrations in Eastern Europe as well as in the United States.

This kaleidoscopic mixture of theory and practice in different countries also seems to suggest that either running public services at a profit, or making them entirely free, or adopting an approach somewhere in between, are all defensible as policy standpoints, no matter what criteria are used to assess them. And such a view is borne out by looking at some of the arguments that have come up in discussions of pricing policy. In the United Kingdom there is a commonly expressed view that a change from a public transport system in which passengers pay for a high proportion of the operating costs through fares, to one which is heavily subsidised by the taxpayer on revenue account, would result in less money being available for maintaining and improving the system: thus leading to a severe decline in the quality of the service offered to the public. This was an argument which also came up in the conflict between Bevan and the doctors about the National Health Service. But it is not difficult to find practical examples both to support and refute that claim. Further, as we have seen in Chapter 3, it is perfectly possible for the relevant governing bodies to either increase, reduce, or maintain service levels, whether the resulting costs are met from taxes, fares, or a mixture between the two.

It is particularly important to note that this line of argument is no more than an opinion about human and institutional behaviour, which can be reasonably and sensibly defended as well as opposed. It should not be confused with the rather different proposition criticised in Chapter 3, that it is 'better' to spend money on service improvements than on fares subsidies. For that comes nearer to being a sophism than a defensible opinion; mainly because it confuses the nature of fares subsidies which should be treated as transfer payments from the taxpayer's to the passenger's pocket, with investments in the system itself that are concerned with how real resources of land, labour, equipment and materials should be deployed so as to create new or improved services.

If we turn to wider issues concerning the impact on society of different pricing policies, it is still not easy to see where the boundary line should be drawn. In favour of free education and health it could be said that this is the best way of raising the community's general educational and health standards, with the resulting beneficial impact on economic efficiency as well as on social welfare. But it could equally be maintained that the same benefits could be won more effectively by making everyone pay the full price for the services bought, with special refunds allowed for identified

150

people in need. Similar arguments can be used both for and against the provision of free public transport. And the decision taken will depend on opinions about matters like social stigma and the administrative problems of devising effective systems of identification, without any conclusive evidence being available to clinch the issue one way or another. Few people will be confident enough to give a resounding judgement of the kind made by the Duke of Wellington, who is reported to have said that third class fares were 'a premium to the lower orders to go uselessly wandering about the country'.

Another argument in favour of free travel is the beneficial impact it would have on reducing traffic congestion and associated environmental pollution. But here again it could be said that it would be possible to obtain similar benefits more effectively by other means. The most obvious alternative is to make car drivers pay more, instead of allowing public transport passengers to pay less; and this could in theory be achieved in a number of ways such as by a road pricing scheme, or through a system under which special supplementary licences have to be bought before a car can be driven in peak periods in the congested parts of the city.[1] It could, however, be argued that some way of increasing the relative costs of private motoring must be found whatever happens to public transport fares. For otherwise the gap between the costs of public and private transport could continue to accelerate at too fast a pace, due to the high proportion of the public transport industry's costs that is accounted for by labour (a problem that will persist except under the most radical programmes of automated transport technology which are not likely to be seen on any scale for some time), compared with the situation in private motoring where the car driver gives his services free of charge.

Thus fares policy decisions are not written on tablets of stone, and it cannot be 'proved' that any one approach is better than another. Decisions must in the end be determined primarily as acts of political judgement; which for the more radical decisions, requires politicians to have the nerve and courage either to bring forward or to reverse the process of social and political evolution that has affected other public services in the past.

7.3 Management procedures

Ideally, however, such essays in political judgement should take place within a clear management framework designed to assist the taking, controlling and monitoring of all the main political decisions, their various consequences, and the management and operational measures that are needed to support them. The essentially qualitative nature of the ultimate political decisions also makes it all the more important to ensure that the decision making processes leading up to them are as rational and consistent as possible, pay careful attention to facts, and allow for learning from experience and for flexible responses to changing conditions.

Such a management system should, as a start, actively encourage decision makers to base their political judgements on the relative importance they attach to a wide range of objectives, and on the evidence that is available about the extent to which different policies might contribute to those objectives. Moreover, if this process leads to a fares policy decision anywhere in between the free and profit maximising extremes, the monitoring and control of the chosen policy would be assisted by the selfregulating procedure suggested in Chapter 3 for determining the amount of subsidy to be paid each year, according to an index related to the rate of inflation. More generally, public transport should be planned and managed as a social service industry, according to the five principles summarised at the end of that chapter.

The main influences over the public transport operators' performance will, of course, continue to come from having to deal with practical management problems such as traffic congestion, breakdowns, accidents, shortages of vehicles and spare parts, and the personnel management and industrial relations facts of life. Similarly, the elected representatives on the local councils will go on having to cope with the very different but no less real political dramas and tensions that are an unavoidable part of their management responsibilities. But this does not make it any the less important to try to build an overall framework for the management of public transport, with the aim of getting the best of both worlds: the sharpness and efficiency of commercial management, as well as the sensitivity and awareness required for the development of effective social policies.

An approach on these lines could in theory be applied to any public service which it has been decided to provide so that it is paid for partly by consumers and partly by government subsidy. Housing is a good example of such a service in the United Kingdom. The approach would, of course, have to be adapted to take account of the jumble of rent restrictions, controlled tenancies, subsidies and tax reliefs that affect both the public and private sectors. But with the relaxation of the controls over council house rents that followed the introduction of the Housing Rents and Subsidies Act in 1975, local authorities are in a position to adopt at least the elements of the management procedures suggested in Chapter 3.

Among other things, this would enable local councils to make positive triangular choices each year about the balance to be struck between rent increases, higher subsidies, and service levels. A systematic and comprehensive management framework is particularly needed because of the sharp and haphazard increase in subsidy levels in recent years (rent income is estimated to have dropped from some three quarters of the running costs of council housing in 1968 to just over one half in 1975), together with the problems caused by local authorities' spiralling capital debts for the houses they buy and build. As with public transport, this latter point also makes it important for the regular reviews of service levels to aim as a first priority at getting the most out of the existing stock of dwellings in both the public and private sectors, through more effective management, maintenance and modernisation programmes.

Because of inflation, virtually any approach to fares policy, apart from free travel, will require the operator to implement regular increases in fares so as to fill the gap between costs and subsidy. For even a policy which involves maintaining fares at their current money levels will soon lead to a situation in which fares income will account for such a small proportion of total costs, that the cost savings resulting from a switch to free travel would be bound to be high enough to justify such a move. Chapter 4 has suggested some practical tools which the operator might use to determine by how much fares should be increased each year, in the light of the expected subsidy from the controlling political authority and of the impact of inflation on costs.

The deep rooted philosophical disagreements about fare levels apply with much less force to fare structures, whose effects are often more easily discernible, and which involve more basic management issues (such as bus operating and fare collection practices) on which it is easier to reach a consensus. However, the main disadvantage of the simplest fare structure, the flat fare, lies in its inflexibility and inefficiency as an instrument for raising increasing amounts of money from passengers. This suggests that decisions on fare level rather than fare structure are of prior importance in fares policy; and that a comparatively low fare level, heavily subsidised from public funds, is a necessary (but not, of course, a sufficient) condition for a flat fare.

This is confirmed by the general review in Chapter 5 of fares policy practices round the world, which not only showed the strength and generality of the movement towards more heavily subsidised public transport services, but also that this has been paralleled by an equally powerful movement towards the adoption of flat fare structures. If the pressures of continuing inflation create a tendency to accept regular fare

153

increases, at least in money terms, as a normal part of life, there may well be a reversal of this latter trend, and a search either for compromises based on coarsely graduated fare structures, or for more radical zonal fares solutions. There are, however, powerful forces working in the opposite direction, such as the political pressures towards lower fare levels, as well as the continual erosion of the ability to raise money from passengers which is resulting from the wider introduction of special concessions.

7.4　The public interest

The detailed analysis in Chapter 6 reveals some important evidence about the social implications of changes in policy on both fare structure and fare level. In the British context it is a widely held view that both the introduction of a low bus flat fare, and a switch in the financing of public transport from fares to rates, are regressive policies in that they lead to undesirable redistributions of income from poor to rich people. But neither of these propositions seems to be correct. On the first point, it appears that richer households use public transport more often than poorer, but do not travel longer distances by bus. Hence a change in fare structure to a low bus flat fare would benefit all income groups by similar proportionate amounts. Further, a low fare level would benefit the poorer households by releasing the considerable pent up demand for extra trip making that appears to exist below a certain income level.

As far as overall financing policy is concerned, it has been shown that higher bus fares are even more regressive than higher rates in their impact, and higher rail fares somewhat less. Although this conclusion is based on evidence for London, the similarity in travel behaviour in relation to income in other British cities suggests that free bus travel is the most progressive fares policy they could adopt, even if it were financed entirely out of the rates. Such a policy would be still more progressive if financed from central rather than local taxation, i.e. by central government grant; which means that the British government has adopted a contrary approach to income distribution through its stated intention to get the bus services back towards a position of commercial viability.

These conclusions must, of course, be treated cautiously for the several reasons given in Chapter 6. Moreover, even though free bus travel financed out of national taxation seems to make the best contribution to the objective of redistributing income from rich to poor people, some policy makers may not agree that this is a desirable objective for public policy. And many of those who do support this aim may feel that it should be tackled directly through national fiscal policies rather than indirectly via subsidising public transport; or that the gains against it which result from free bus travel are insufficient to offset adverse contributions to other objectives. Nevertheless, the conclusions do as a minimum confirm once more that there is a perfectly respectable case for heavy subsidisation of public transport services, and even for free bus travel, which cannot be dismissed out of hand.

Such policies can only be considered seriously, however, if it is recognised that the large sums of money required for their implementation should be treated as transfers of money from the taxpayer which do not in themselves make direct claims on real resources; and that it is primarily those expenditures which make such direct claims which may have to be restrained in periods of economic recession. Such restrictions should affect particularly the large scale capital investments that have tended to dominate the transport planning process until fairly recently. Priority has to be given instead to those solutions to the urban transport problem which obtain the greatest improvements to the service offered to the public for the smallest claim on real resources.

However, although those fares policies which give rise to income transfers should be considered in a different way to investments in the system which make direct claims on real resources, the review of experience round the world has highlighted the importance of developing integrated transport strategies which take account of the close inter-dependence of the effects on the travelling public of both types of policy. The right package of fare level, fare structure and special concessions, together with the appropriate traffic restraint measures, service improvements, and so on, has to be chosen in the light of their combined effect on social, environmental, financial and economic, and operational aims of the kind listed in Chapter 2.

This requires among other things, a recognition in transport planning procedures of the importance of treating people as far as possible as individuals, with different and sometimes idiosyncratic needs and behaviour patterns. It has been argued elsewhere that such an approach does not fit in easily with traditional transport planning and modelling procedures;[2] and a similar conclusion might be drawn from some of the points made in Chapter 1. Whether or not there is any justice in that charge, it is certainly true that conventional methods need to be supplemented by more flexible analyses which examine directly the social implications of transport policies. Indeed, an economic climate in which priority has to be given to low cost policies with high pay offs, provides a good opportunity to think carefully about how the traditional, large scale, expensive computer based procedures are to be used, and to consider how better value for money might be obtained from cheaper and more flexible analytical routines that get closer to the heart of the most critical decision problems.

But whatever analytical procedures are used to assess alternative fares policies, it would be unwise to be over confident about predicting the effects of those which are likely to have the most powerful influences on society, such as free travel for everybody. For they are well outside the realms of our current experience and there is no empirical evidence available to test directly their dynamic effects. Further, they could become part of a wider process of social, political and institutional evolution involving significant departures from current behaviour patterns.

Thus in line with the remarks made earlier, we cannot be certain whether people on average will be better or worse off under radically different fare levels and structures. But this makes it even more important to analyse the underlying situation as carefully and objectively as possible, in order to help provide the insights and evidence for the formulation of the political judgements on which decisions will primarily depend.

Notes

[1] Such a scheme for London has been outlined in the GLC's discussion document *Supplementary Licensing,* issued in 1975.

[2] M. Hillman, I. Henderson, A. Whalley, *Personal Mobility and Transport Policy,* Political and Economic Planning, 1973.

156

Index

The Author

After an initial career as a teacher Alexander Grey joined the civil service to work in the Treasury and later in the Department of Economic Affairs. He then left public service to become a consultant economist, specialising in regional planning and commodities. In 1970 he joined the Director-General's Department of the Greater London Council to help set up a new system of corporate management. Since 1973 he has been Head of the Public Transport Division of the Greater London Council Planning and Transportation Department.